EXPLORING THE INTERSECTION OF
ARTIFICIAL INTELLIGENCE AND CYBER DEFENSE

STEPHEN NNAMDI

Copyright © 2023. All rights reserved. Stephen Nnamdi

No part of this book may be reproduced or transmitted in any form or by any means, electronic or mechanical, including photocopying, recording, or by any information storage and retrieval system, without permission in writing from the Copyright owner.

Any information is to be used for educational and information purposes only. It should never be substituted for financial advice.

The author or publisher does not in any way endorse any commercial products or services linked from other websites to this book.

ISBN: 978-2-9739-4318-8

PREFACE

This book investigates the transformative impact of AI technologies on modern cybersecurity practices. It starts by laying the foundation of artificial intelligence, explaining key concepts and how AI is applied to enhance threat detection and response. A detailed look at how machine learning algorithms and other AI techniques are revolutionizing the way cyber threats are identified and managed are examined.

It delves into various AI-driven approaches to improving cyber defense, such as automating incident response, predictive analytics, and behavioral analysis. It highlights the role of the technology in identifying vulnerabilities and mitigating sophisticated attacks, including zero-day exploits. Through practical examples and case studies, it illustrates how AI tools can be integrated into existing security frameworks to bolster defenses and streamline operations.

In its final chapters, the book addresses the ethical and privacy concerns associated with AI in cybersecurity, emphasizing the need for a balanced approach. It also explores its future in cyber defense, discussing emerging trends and potential challenges. By providing a comprehensive overview of AI's role in enhancing cybersecurity, we offer valuable insights into how thus technology can be leveraged to create more resilient security systems.

TABLE OF CONTENT

PREFACE iii
TABLE OF CONTENT iv
DEDICATION vi

1. AI IN CYBER DEFENSE 1
   Understanding Artificial Intelligence 2
   Challenges and Considerations 7

2. THE BASICS OF ARTIFICIAL INTELLIGENCE: CONCEPTS AND TERMINOLOGY 13
   Defining Artificial Intelligence 13
   Fundamental AI Techniques and Methods 17
   Applications of AI 21

3. AI-DRIVEN THREAT DETECTION 27
   The Role of AI and ML in Threat Detection 28
   Challenges and Considerations 31

4. AUTOMATING INCIDENT RESPONSE 35
   Understanding Incident Response 35
   Benefits and Disadvantages of AI-Driven Incident Response 38
   Implementing AI-Driven Incident Response 41

5. BEHAVIORAL ANALYSIS AND ANOMALY DETECTION 43
   What is Behavioral Analysis and Anomaly Detection 43
   Real-World Applications 48

6. PREDICTIVE ANALYTICS IN CYBERSECURITY 53
   Understanding Predictive Analytics 53
   Applications of Predictive Analytics in Cybersecurity 56
   Real-World Case Studies and Applications 57

7. THE ROLE OF AI IN IDENTIFYING AND MITIGATING ZERO- DAY EXPLOITS 63
What is Zero-Day Exploits 63
AI-Based Mitigation Strategies for Zero-Day Exploits and Case Studies 68
Case Studies: AI in Action Against Zero-Day Exploits 69

8. AI POWERED THREAT INTELLIGENCE 73
The Role and Application of AI in Threat Intelligence 74
Benefits and Drawbacks of AI-Powered Threat Intelligence 77
Case Study: Evaluating an AI-Powered Threat Intelligence Solution 83

9. ETHICAL AND PRIVACY CONCERNS: BALANCING AI WITH USER RIGHTS 85
Understanding AI and Its Capabilities 85
Balancing AI Use with User Rights 89
Legal and Regulatory Frameworks for AI Ethics and Privacy 92
The Impact of AI on Social Justice and Equity 94

10. AI AND HUMAN COLLABORATION 97
AI and Human Functions in Defense Frameworks 97
Synergizing AI and Human Strategies 101

11. INTEGRATING AI INTO CYBER DEFENSE: KEY TAKEAWAYS AND FUTURE DIRECTIONS 107
Key Takeaways 107
Practical Applications of AI in Cyber Defense 111

ABOUT THE AUTHOR 117

DEDICATION

To those who tirelessly push the boundaries of innovation, your relentless pursuit of knowledge and advancement inspires every page of this work. This book is dedicated to the pioneers of both artificial intelligence and cyber defense who navigate the complexities of these fields with unwavering determination and curiosity. Your passion for safeguarding our digital future and your commitment to advancing intelligent technologies are the driving forces behind the exploration contained within these pages.

To the unsung heroes working in the shadows, often unnoticed, who confront threats and vulnerabilities with courage and ingenuity—this book is a testament to your dedication. Your efforts, though sometimes behind the scenes, are crucial in protecting the fabric of our interconnected world. The intersection of AI and cyber defense is a testament to your relentless vigilance and creativity in addressing the ever-evolving challenges of our digital age.

To those who dare to envision the future and challenge the status quo, this work is dedicated to your boldness. The fusion of artificial intelligence with cyber defense is not merely a technical convergence but a reflection of the audacity required to redefine how we approach security and intelligence. Your innovative spirit and forward-thinking mindset are the cornerstones upon which this exploration is built.

Finally, to the readers and learners who embark on this journey through the realms of AI and cyber defense, may you find in these pages both insight and inspiration. This book is dedicated to the collective effort of understanding and harnessing the power of technology to create a safer, more resilient digital landscape. Your engagement with this material is a step towards a future where intelligence and security coexist harmoniously.

1. AI IN CYBER DEFENSE

In the contemporary digital sphere, cybersecurity is no longer just an IT concern but a critical component of national security, economic stability, and personal privacy. The exponential growth in data generation, the increasing sophistication of cyber-attacks, and the expanding surface area of potential vulnerabilities have escalated the need for robust and adaptive cyber defense mechanisms. Traditional approaches, while foundational, often struggle to keep pace with the dynamic nature of cyber threats. This scenario creates a fertile ground for the integration of Artificial Intelligence (AI) into cyber defense strategies.

Cyber threats today are not only more numerous but also more complex. Attackers employ advanced techniques such as AI-powered malware, social engineering, and polymorphic viruses that can evade traditional detection methods. The traditional rule-based systems and signature-based approaches, while still relevant, are often insufficient in recognizing novel or sophisticated attacks. This gap has led to the exploration and adoption of AI technologies to enhance threat detection, response, and overall security posture.

Understanding Artificial Intelligence

Artificial Intelligence (AI) refers to the simulation of human intelligence in machines designed to perform tasks that typically require human cognitive processes. AI encompasses a broad range of technologies including machine learning (ML), natural language processing (NLP), and neural networks. In the context of cyber defense, AI can be used to automate tasks, improve threat detection, and even predict potential attacks.

Machine Learning (ML): ML algorithms enable systems to learn from data and improve their performance over time without being explicitly programmed. In cybersecurity, ML can be employed to identify patterns and anomalies that signify potential threats, making it a crucial tool for adaptive defense mechanisms.

Natural Language Processing (NLP): NLP involves the interaction between computers and human languages. In cyber defense, NLP can be utilized to analyze and understand large volumes of textual data from various sources, such as security logs and threat intelligence feeds, to extract actionable insights.

Neural Networks: These are computational models inspired by the human brain's neural architecture. Neural networks, particularly deep learning models, have shown significant promise in identifying complex patterns in large datasets, which is invaluable for detecting sophisticated cyber threats.

Computer Vision: Computer Vision involves the use of AI to interpret and understand visual information from the world. In cybersecurity, computer vision can be employed to analyze video feeds from security cameras, monitor physical access points, and identify suspicious activities or behaviors. For example, AI-powered computer vision systems can detect unauthorized personnel entering secure areas or recognize unusual patterns in surveillance footage, providing an additional layer of security to physical and cyber environments.

Robotic Process Automation (RPA): This involves the use of AI-driven software robots or "bots" to automate repetitive and rule-based tasks. In this context, RPA can streamline routine tasks such as data collection, log analysis, and incident response. For example, RPA can be used to automate the process of aggregating and analyzing security logs from multiple sources, applying predefined rules to identify potential threats, and generating reports. This automation frees up human analysts to focus on more complex and strategic tasks, improving overall efficiency and response times.

Expert Systems: Expert Systems are applications that mimic the decision-making abilities of human experts. These systems use a knowledge base of expert-level information and inference rules to solve complex problems and provide recommendations. Here, expert systems can be used to develop advanced threat detection and response strategies by leveraging a repository of security knowledge and best practices. For example, an expert system could assist in identifying potential vulnerabilities, suggesting remediation steps based on known attack patterns, and providing guidance on incident management based on historical data and expert input.

As cybersecurity threats become increasingly sophisticated, Artificial Intelligence (AI) emerges as a crucial component in modern defense strategies. By leveraging advanced algorithms and data-driven insights, AI offers innovative solutions to complex security challenges.

AI has the potential to revolutionize cyber defense in several key areas. Traditional cybersecurity systems often rely on predefined rules and signatures to detect threats, which can be limiting as threats evolve. In contrast, AI-powered systems excel at analyzing vast amounts of data in real-time to identify anomalous patterns that may indicate potential threats. For instance, machine learning (ML) algorithms can learn from historical attack data, allowing them to recognize and adapt to new types of malware or phishing attempts that were previously unknown. This ability to detect and analyze emerging threats provides a significant advantage in maintaining robust and adaptive security defenses.

Automated response systems can significantly enhance response times by taking over routine tasks such as incident analysis and remediation. These systems can swiftly isolate affected systems, apply patches, and mitigate attacks without requiring human intervention, thereby reducing the time attackers have to exploit vulnerabilities and minimizing the impact of breaches. Additionally, predictive capabilities enable proactive threat management by analyzing trends and historical data to forecast potential future attacks and vulnerabilities. This foresight allows organizations to implement preventive measures before an attack occurs, effectively shifting the focus from reactive to proactive defense.

Adaptive learning represents a key advantage in cybersecurity, as it allows systems to continuously evolve and enhance their capabilities. These systems can learn from new data and adapt their detection and response strategies in real time as threats change. This ongoing learning process improves the system's ability to manage emerging threats and reduces the need for frequent manual updates.

In addition, threat intelligence aggregation benefits significantly from advanced technology. Traditional methods of gathering and analyzing threat intelligence can be slow and prone to errors due to their manual nature. By automating the collection and integration of data from diverse sources—such as threat feeds, security logs, and social media—advanced systems can provide a more comprehensive view of the threat landscape. Utilizing techniques like natural language processing and machine learning, these systems can identify relevant threats, correlate data points, and offer valuable insights. This enhanced aggregation of intelligence enables security teams to stay informed about emerging threats and trends, improving their ability to respond effectively.

Behavioral analytics significantly improve the detection of insider threats by monitoring and analyzing patterns in user behavior. AI systems establish a baseline of normal activity based on how individuals typically interact with systems and data. When deviations from this baseline occur such as unusual access to sensitive information or irregular login times, the system can automatically flag these anomalies for further scrutiny. This method enhances the ability to detect potential insider threats that might circumvent traditional security measures, thereby reducing the risk of data breaches resulting from malicious or careless insider actions.

AI can provide contextual analysis of cyber threats by understanding the specific environment and context in which they occur. Contextual analysis involves examining the environment, such as network architecture, organizational policies, and recent security events, to understand the relevance and potential impact of a threat. AI systems can correlate threat indicators with contextual information to determine the severity and potential consequences of an attack. This helps prioritize responses and allocate resources more effectively, ensuring that the most critical threats are addressed promptly.

It can bolster endpoint protection by providing advanced capabilities for detecting and responding to threats at the device level. Current endpoint protection solutions often rely on signature-based detection, which can be inadequate for identifying new or sophisticated threats. AI-powered endpoint protection systems utilize machine learning to monitor processes, network activity, and file behavior in real-time. By analyzing these activities, it can identify malicious behavior and respond autonomously by isolating affected endpoints, preventing further spread of malware, and initiating remediation actions. This improves the overall security posture by ensuring that endpoints are continuously monitored and protected.

Dynamic risk assessment and management can be greatly enhanced through continuous evaluation and adjustment of an organization's risk posture. Conventional risk assessment methods are often static and periodic, potentially overlooking changes in the threat landscape. By analyzing factors such as network vulnerabilities, threat intelligence, and system configurations in real time, advanced systems can provide up-to-date risk assessments. Incorporating real-time data and predictive analytics enables these systems to adjust risk scores dynamically and suggest appropriate mitigation strategies. This approach allows organizations to proactively manage their risk profile and respond more effectively to emerging threats.

Challenges and Considerations

While AI offers numerous benefits for cyber defense, it also introduces several challenges and considerations:

Data Privacy and Security: The use of AI in cybersecurity often involves analyzing large volumes of sensitive data. Ensuring that this data is handled securely and that privacy is maintained is crucial. These systems must be designed to comply with data protection regulations and to protect against potential misuse.

False Positives and Negatives: AI systems, particularly those based on machine learning, are not infallible. They can produce false positives (incorrectly identifying benign activity as malicious) or false negatives (failing to detect actual threats). Balancing sensitivity and specificity is essential to minimize these errors and ensure that security teams can effectively respond to real threats.

Complexity and Integration: Implementing this technology in existing security frameworks can be complex. Integrating solutions with legacy systems and ensuring that they work seamlessly with other security tools requires careful planning and expertise. Organizations must also invest in training their staff to effectively utilize and manage AI-powered systems.

Ethical and Legal Implications: The use of AI in cyber defense raises ethical and legal questions. For example, the deployment of autonomous systems for threat mitigation might lead to unintended consequences or collateral damage. Organizations must consider the ethical implications of its decision-making and ensure that their use adheres to legal and ethical standards.

Resource and Cost Implications: Implementing and maintaining AI-driven cybersecurity solutions can entail significant resource and cost implications. These frameworks often require substantial computational power, storage, and specialized hardware, which can be expensive to acquire and operate. Additionally, the development, training, and fine-tuning of the models necessitate skilled personnel with expertise in data science and machine learning. Organizations must also account for ongoing maintenance, updates, and potential scalability issues as the volume of data and complexity of threats increase. Balancing the costs of these advanced technologies with the need for effective security measures can be a challenge, particularly for smaller organizations with limited budgets.

Over-reliance on AI Systems: An over-reliance on these systems in security can pose risks, particularly if human oversight is minimized or neglected. While the technology can significantly enhance threat detection and response capabilities, it is not infallible and can sometimes produce incorrect results or miss subtle threats. Relying solely on the technology without adequate human intervention may lead to vulnerabilities or delayed responses to emerging threats. It is crucial to maintain a balance between AI-driven automation and human expertise, ensuring that security teams are actively engaged in oversight, decision-making, and contextual analysis. Developing a robust incident response plan that integrates both AI and human elements can help mitigate the risks associated with over-reliance on automated systems.

The future of AI in cyber defense promises to bring transformative advancements as technology continues to evolve. Emerging innovations and evolving applications will redefine how we approach threat detection, response, and overall cybersecurity strategy.

The integration of these technology into cyber defense is an ongoing and evolving process. As technology advances, AI systems will become more sophisticated, providing even greater capabilities for threat detection and response. The future trends will likely involve increased collaboration between human and machine intelligence, leveraging the strengths of both to create more resilient and adaptive defense mechanisms. The development of new emerging technologies, such as quantum computing and advanced neural networks, will further enhance security capabilities. These technologies hold the promise of solving complex problems and improving the efficiency and effectiveness of cyber defense strategies.

Collaboration and sharing between organizations, governments, and the cybersecurity community will be crucial in advancing AI-driven defense mechanisms. Sharing threat intelligence and best practices can help organizations stay ahead of emerging threats and leverage collective knowledge to improve overall security. The dynamic nature of cyber threats necessitates a continuous improvement approach to learning this technology particularly as relates to cyber defense. Ongoing research, development, and adaptation will be essential in ensuring that AI systems remain effective in the face of evolving threats.

The future of AI in cyber defense will also likely see significant advancements through the integration with quantum computing. Quantum computers have the potential to solve complex problems at speeds that are orders of magnitude faster than classical computers. This capability could revolutionize cryptographic techniques, enhance threat modeling, and accelerate the processing of vast amounts of security data. Quantum-enhanced AI systems could provide unprecedented accuracy in threat detection and prediction, as well as offer more robust defense mechanisms against quantum-enabled attacks. Preparing for the implications of quantum computing will be crucial for future-proofing security strategies.

As the technology progresses, we can anticipate the development of fully autonomous cyber defense systems capable of independently managing and mitigating threats. These systems would leverage advanced machine learning algorithms and real-time data to make decisions and execute defensive actions without human intervention. Autonomous systems could dynamically adjust security postures, apply patches, and respond to incidents in real-time, reducing response times and potentially improving overall security. However, this evolution will also necessitate robust safeguards to ensure that autonomous decisions align with organizational policies and do not inadvertently cause collateral damage.

Finally, as AI becomes more central to security measures, addressing ethical considerations and mitigating biases in the systems will be crucial. Ensuring that these algorithms are transparent, fair, and free from biases is essential for maintaining trust and effectiveness in cyber defense. We will likely see increased focus on developing ethical frameworks and guidelines to govern the use of it in security applications. This includes implementing practices to regularly audit AI models for biases, ensuring diverse data representation, and establishing clear accountability for decisions delivered. Ethical considerations will play a key role in shaping the responsible and equitable use of the technology in protecting digital assets.

The convergence of artificial intelligence and cyber defense marks a significant shift in our approach to cybersecurity. Leveraging this advanced technology enables organizations to improve their capabilities in detecting, responding to, and preventing cyber threats. Nonetheless, integrating these solutions introduces challenges that need to be overcome to fully unlock their potential in securing our digital sector. Moving forward, the synergy between human expertise and machine intelligence will be crucial for creating a secure and resilient cyberspaces.

2. THE BASICS OF ARTIFICIAL INTELLIGENCE: CONCEPTS AND TERMINOLOGY

Artificial Intelligence (AI) represents one of the progressive technological advancements of the modern era. It encompasses a broad range of technologies and methodologies designed to enable machines to perform tasks that would typically require human intelligence. From self-driving cars to voice-activated assistants, this technology is increasingly becoming an integral part of our daily lives. This chapter delves into the fundamental concepts and terminology that underpin AI, providing a comprehensive overview of its core principles, key technologies, and the evolving direction of this innovative field.

Defining Artificial Intelligence

AI is a field of computer science dedicated to creating systems that can perform tasks requiring human-like cognitive functions. These tasks include reasoning, learning, problem-solving, perception, and language understanding. The primary goal of AI is to develop machines that can mimic or exceed human capabilities in these areas. It can be categorized into two broad types namely Strong AI and Weak AI.

Strong AI, also known as Artificial General Intelligence (AGI), refers to systems that possess the ability to understand, learn, and apply intelligence across a broad range of tasks at a level comparable to human cognition. Strong AI is theoretical at this point, as no existing systems exhibit true AGI. Weak AI, or Narrow AI, refers to systems designed to perform specific tasks or solve particular problems. These systems are specialized and lack the general cognitive abilities of Strong AI. Examples include voice assistants like Siri or Alexa, and recommendation systems used by streaming services.

AI is an umbrella term that encompasses various subfields, including Machine Learning (ML) and Deep Learning (DL). Machine Learning (ML) is a subset that involves the development of algorithms that allow systems to learn from and make predictions or decisions based on data. ML algorithms improve their performance over time as they are exposed to more data. ML encompasses various approaches, including supervised learning, unsupervised learning, and reinforcement learning. Deep Learning (DL) is a subset of Machine Learning that employs neural networks with many layers (hence "deep") to analyze complex patterns in large datasets. DL models are particularly effective in tasks such as image and speech recognition. They have achieved significant advancements in various domains due to their ability to automatically learn features from raw data.

Understanding this technology properly requires familiarity with several core concepts and terminologies.

Algorithms and Models: An algorithm is a step-by-step procedure or formula for solving a problem. In the context of AI, algorithms are used to process data, make decisions, and learn from experience.

Common algorithms include decision trees, support vector machines, and clustering algorithms. A model on the other hand is a mathematical representation of a real-world process or system that is used to make predictions or decisions. In ML, models are trained on data to recognize patterns and make inferences. For example, a classification model might be trained to distinguish between spam and non-spam emails.

Training and Testing: Training refers to the process of teaching an AI model to recognize patterns or make decisions by exposing it to a dataset. During training, the model adjusts its parameters to minimize errors and improve accuracy. This process involves using algorithms to optimize the model's performance based on the training data. Testing involves evaluating the performance of a trained model using a separate dataset that was not used during the training phase. This helps assess the model's ability to generalize to new, unseen data and ensures that it performs well in real-world scenarios.

Data and Features: Data is the raw input used by AI systems to learn and make predictions. In AI, data can come in various forms, including text, images, audio, and numerical values. The quality and quantity of data significantly impact the performance of AI models. Features are the individual measurable properties or characteristics used by a model to make predictions. For example, in a model predicting house prices, features might include the number of bedrooms, square footage, and location.

Core technologies in AI form the foundation of intelligent systems, enabling them to learn, adapt, and perform complex tasks. These technologies encompass a range of methodologies and tools that drive advancements in machine learning, natural language processing, and other key areas of artificial intelligence. They include:

Natural Language Processing (NLP): This is a field of AI focused on enabling machines to understand, interpret, and generate human language. It encompasses a range of tasks. Text analysis involves extracting meaningful information from textual data, such as through sentiment analysis or named entity recognition. Machine translation enables the automatic conversion of text from one language to another, facilitating cross-linguistic communication. Speech recognition technology converts spoken language into written text, enhancing accessibility and interaction with digital systems. Additionally, language generation techniques produce coherent and contextually relevant text, which is utilized in applications such as chatbots and automated content creation.

Computer Vision: It involves enabling machines to interpret and understand visual information from the world. For instance, image classification involves assigning labels to images based on their content, such as identifying specific objects or scenes. Object detection extends this capability by locating and identifying individual objects within an image. Image segmentation further refines analysis by dividing an image into distinct segments, such as separating the foreground from the background, to facilitate more detailed and precise examination.

Robotics: Robotics integrates AI with physical machines to perform tasks in the real world. AI-driven robotics can be used for various applications and services. Industrial automation involves the use of robots to perform repetitive tasks in manufacturing and assembly processes, enhancing efficiency and precision. In the medical field, robotics assist with surgeries and patient care, providing advanced support and improving outcomes. Service robots, on the other hand, are designed for tasks in homes or public spaces, such as cleaning or delivery, contributing to convenience and operational effectiveness in various environments.

Expert Systems: These are applications designed to mimic the decision-making abilities of human experts in specific domains. They use a knowledge base of rules and facts to provide recommendations or solutions. Expert systems are used in various fields, including medical diagnosis, financial forecasting, and troubleshooting.

Fundamental AI Techniques and Methods

Understanding the core techniques and methods in Artificial Intelligence (AI) is essential for grasping how AI systems are designed, trained, and deployed. This section delves into some of the fundamental techniques and methods that form the backbone of the technology, providing insight into how they work and their applications.

Machine Learning (ML): It is a subset that focuses on developing algorithms that enable computers to learn from and make predictions based on data. Supervised learning is a primary technique within machine learning where algorithms are trained on labeled data, with each input paired with the correct output. The model learns to map inputs to outputs by minimizing the error between its predictions and the actual results. Common algorithms used in supervised learning include linear regression, logistic regression, and support vector machines. This technique is widely applied in various domains, such as email spam filtering and image classification, where it enables accurate prediction and classification based on historical data.

Unsupervised learning involves training algorithms on unlabeled data, where the system seeks to identify patterns and structures without predefined labels. This technique includes clustering methods, such as K-means clustering, and dimensionality reduction methods, such as Principal Component Analysis (PCA). Applications of unsupervised learning encompass tasks like customer segmentation and feature extraction. Reinforcement learning, on the other hand, involves an agent that learns to make decisions by receiving rewards or penalties based on its actions. The objective is to develop a policy that maximizes cumulative rewards over time. Key algorithms in reinforcement learning include Q-learning and deep Q-networks (DQN), with applications in robotics and game playing.

Neural Networks: Neural Networks are computational models inspired by the human brain's structure and function. They consist of interconnected nodes (neurons) organized into layers. Feedforward Neural Networks (FNNs) are the simplest type of neural network where information moves in one direction, from input to output. They are used for tasks like pattern recognition and function approximation.

Convolutional Neural Networks (CNNs) are specialized neural networks designed for processing structured grid data, such as images. They use convolutional layers to detect features and pooling layers to reduce dimensionality. CNNs are widely used in image and video recognition. Recurrent Neural Networks (RNNs) are designed for sequential data and can maintain a memory of previous inputs. They are used in applications like natural language processing and time series forecasting. Variants include Long Short-Term Memory (LSTM) networks and Gated Recurrent Units (GRUs).

Natural Language Processing (NLP): Natural Language Processing (NLP) focuses on enabling computers to understand, interpret, and generate human language. Key techniques in natural language processing include tokenization and part-of-speech tagging. Tokenization involves splitting text into individual tokens, such as words or phrases, to facilitate subsequent analysis and processing. Part-of-speech tagging, on the other hand, identifies the grammatical categories of words within a sentence, such as nouns, verbs, and adjectives, to understand their roles and relationships within the text.

Named Entity Recognition (NER) involves extracting and classifying named entities from text, such as people, organizations, and locations, to provide structured and actionable information. Machine translation refers to the automatic translation of text from one language to another using models trained on bilingual corpora. This technique encompasses methods like statistical machine translation and neural machine translation, which facilitate accurate and contextually relevant translations across different languages.

Optimization Algorithms: These are used to improve the performance of AI models by finding the best parameters or solutions. Gradient Descent is a popular optimization technique used to minimize the loss function of machine learning models. It involves iteratively adjusting model parameters in the direction of the steepest decrease in the loss function. Genetic Algorithms is inspired by the process of natural selection, genetic algorithms use techniques such as mutation, crossover, and selection to evolve solutions to optimization problems. They are used in scenarios where traditional methods are impractical. Simulated Annealing refers to an optimization technique that mimics the annealing process in metallurgy. It involves probabilistically accepting worse solutions to escape local minima and gradually converging to an optimal solution.

Data Preprocessing: Data preprocessing is a crucial step that prepares raw data for analysis and modeling. Data Cleaning involves removing or correcting errors and inconsistencies in the data to ensure its quality and accuracy. Techniques include handling missing values, outlier detection, and data normalization. Feature Engineering refers to creating new features or modifying existing ones to improve the performance of machine learning models. This process involves selecting relevant features, transforming data, and generating new variables. Finally, data augmentation is the expanding the training dataset by applying transformations such as rotation, scaling, and cropping to increase the diversity of data and improve model generalization. This is particularly useful in image and text data.

Evaluation Metrics: These are used to assess the performance of AI models and determine their effectiveness. Accuracy is a metric that represents the proportion of correctly classified instances out of the total instances, commonly used to assess performance in classification tasks. Precision and recall are additional metrics used to evaluate classification models, particularly in cases of imbalanced datasets. Precision measures the proportion of true positive predictions among all positive predictions made by the model, while recall assesses the proportion of true positive predictions out of all actual positive instances. Together, these metrics provide a more nuanced evaluation of model performance beyond simple accuracy. The F1 score is a metric that combines precision and recall into a single value by calculating their harmonic mean, providing a balanced assessment when both precision and recall are important. This metric is particularly useful in evaluating models where achieving a good trade-off between precision and recall is crucial. Mean Squared Error (MSE), on the other hand, is used for regression tasks to measure the average squared difference between predicted and actual values. MSE helps assess the accuracy of regression models by quantifying the magnitude of prediction errors.

The fundamental techniques and methods in AI, including machine learning algorithms, neural networks, natural language processing, optimization algorithms, data preprocessing, and evaluation metrics, form the foundation of AI technology. Understanding these techniques is crucial for developing, implementing, and improving AI systems. By grasping these core methods, practitioners can better design and apply AI solutions to solve complex problems and drive innovation across various domains.

Applications of AI

There is a wide range of applications across different sectors, each leveraging its capabilities to address specific challenges. In healthcare, it plays a crucial role in enhancing various aspects of patient care. AI systems are employed in diagnostics to analyze medical images, such as X-rays and MRIs, helping to assist in the accurate diagnosis of diseases. Additionally, the algorithms contribute to personalized medicine by analyzing patient data to tailor treatments according to individual needs, thereby improving treatment efficacy and patient outcomes. It can also aid to accelerate the process of discovering new drugs by analyzing large datasets and predicting potential compounds.

In the financial sector, AI applications significantly enhance operational efficiency and security. These systems are utilized for fraud detection by analyzing transaction patterns to identify and prevent fraudulent activities. The algorithmic trading employs the algorithms to analyze market data and execute trades at high speeds, optimizing trading strategies and maximizing returns. It also provides support and handle customer inquiries through AI-powered chatbots and virtual assistants.

It is revolutionizing transportation in several impactful ways. Autonomous vehicles rely on the technology to navigate roads and make driving decisions, enhancing safety and efficiency. These systems are also used in traffic management to optimize traffic flow and reduce congestion, leading to smoother commutes. AI enhances route planning by providing real-time navigation and route optimization for logistics and delivery services, improving operational efficiency and timeliness.

In education, the technology is significantly enhancing the learning experience through various applications. AI systems enable personalized learning by adapting educational materials to meet the unique needs and progress of individual students. It can automate the grading of assignments and provide timely feedback, streamlining the assessment process. Furthermore, AI-powered virtual tutors offer supplementary support and resources, helping students with additional guidance and reinforcing their understanding of the subject matter.

For the retail industry, AI is transforming customer experiences and operational efficiency in several ways. The algorithms enhance personalized recommendations by analyzing customer behavior and purchase history to suggest products that match individual preferences, which boosts the shopping experience and drives sales. Additionally, these systems improve inventory management by predicting demand patterns and optimizing stock levels, thereby minimizing the risks of overstocking or stockouts and enhancing supply chain efficiency. Furthermore, chatbots and virtual assistants streamline customer service by handling inquiries, processing orders, and providing support, leading to a more efficient and responsive service experience.

AI is transforming agriculture through various innovative applications. Precision farming utilizes data from sensors and satellites to optimize planting, watering, and harvesting schedules, resulting in increased crop yields and more efficient use of resources. In pest and disease detection, image recognition tools monitor crops for signs of pests and diseases, enabling timely intervention and reducing reliance on chemical treatments. Also, farm automation involves the use of robots and drones to perform tasks such as planting, weeding, and harvesting, enhancing productivity and lowering labor costs.

In the entertainment industry, AI enhances content creation and user experiences in several impactful ways. Content generation utilizes algorithms to create music, write stories, and produce visual art, offering new avenues for creativity and production. Audience analytics leverages AI to analyze viewer preferences and behaviors, leading to personalized content recommendations on streaming platforms and boosting user engagement and satisfaction. In game development, it contributes to creating adaptive and intelligent non-player characters (NPCs), which enrich gameplay experiences and provide dynamic challenges for players.

For the energy sector, these applications significantly enhance various aspects of operations. Smart grid management utilizes algorithms to optimize the distribution of electricity across smart grids, balancing supply and demand while improving energy efficiency.

Predictive maintenance involves analyzing data from energy infrastructure to forecast and prevent equipment failures, thereby reducing downtime and maintenance costs. Additionally, energy consumption optimization uses advanced systems to monitor and analyze usage patterns in buildings and industrial processes, recommending and implementing measures to reduce overall consumption and costs.

In the security sector, AI enhances various aspects of threat detection and management. Intrusion Detection Systems (IDS) use advanced algorithms to analyze network traffic patterns, identifying unusual or suspicious activities that could signal potential security breaches. These systems, powered by machine learning, offer more effective detection and response to new and evolving threats compared to traditional rule-based methods. They are employed for fraud prevention by analyzing transaction patterns and user behavior to identify fraudulent activities in real time, thus safeguarding sensitive information from unauthorized access. Surveillance and monitoring benefit from AI-driven video analytics, which automatically detect and alert on suspicious behavior, such as unauthorized access or unusual movements, thereby improving the effectiveness of security monitoring and response in various settings.

As AI continues to advance, it raises several ethical and societal considerations:

Bias and Fairness: AI systems can inadvertently perpetuate biases present in the data they are trained on. Ensuring fairness and mitigating bias is crucial to prevent discriminatory outcomes and promote equitable treatment.

Privacy: The collection and use of personal data for applications raise concerns about privacy and data security. Ensuring that AI systems adhere to privacy regulations and protect sensitive information is essential.

Job Displacement: The automation of tasks through AI has the potential to displace certain jobs, leading to economic and social challenges. Addressing the impact on employment and providing support for affected workers is important for a balanced transition.

Accountability: As these systems make more autonomous decisions, determining accountability for their actions becomes increasingly complex. Establishing clear guidelines for responsibility and transparency is necessary to address potential issues.

Artificial Intelligence is a rapidly evolving field with profound implications for technology and society. Understanding the basic concepts and terminology is essential for navigating its complexities and harnessing its potential. As it continues to advance, its applications will expand, presenting new opportunities and challenges. By staying informed about foundational principles, technologies, and ethical considerations, we can better prepare for and contribute to the transformative impact of this ever-changing field.

3. AI-DRIVEN THREAT DETECTION

The traditional methods of threat detection are increasingly proving inadequate against the sophisticated and diverse range of cyber threats showing up on the scene regularly. As cyberattacks become more complex and prevalent, organizations are turning to advanced technologies to bolster their defenses. Among these technologies, Artificial Intelligence (AI) and Machine Learning (ML) have emerged as pivotal tools in enhancing threat detection and response capabilities. This chapter explores how AI-driven threat detection systems are improving cybersecurity, providing insights into their functionalities, benefits, and challenges.

To understand the impact of AI-driven threat detection, it is essential to grasp the evolution of cyber threats. Early cyberattacks were relatively straightforward, often executed by individuals with limited resources. These attacks, such as simple viruses and worms, were relatively easy to detect and mitigate with basic security measures. As technology advanced, so did the complexity of cyber threats. Modern attacks are often carried out by well-funded and highly skilled adversaries, including organized crime groups and nation-state actors. These threats are characterized by their sophistication, persistence, and ability to evade traditional security measures. Techniques such as polymorphic malware, fileless attacks, and advanced persistent threats

(APTs) pose significant challenges to conventional threat detection systems.

The Role of AI and ML in Threat Detection

Artificial Intelligence and Machine Learning are transforming the way organizations approach threat detection. Unlike traditional systems that rely on predefined rules and signatures, AI and ML models are designed to learn from data and adapt to new threats. This ability to analyze vast amounts of data and identify patterns makes AI-driven threat detection particularly effective against evolving and unknown threats.

Machine Learning Algorithms: Machine Learning algorithms are at the heart of AI-driven threat detection. These algorithms are trained on large datasets to recognize patterns and anomalies that may indicate a security threat. Common ML techniques used in threat detection include supervised learning, unsupervised learning, and reinforcement learning. In supervised learning, algorithms are trained on labeled data, where each data point is associated with a known outcome. For example, a supervised learning model might be trained on historical data of known threats and non-threats to learn the characteristics of different attack types. Once trained, the model can then classify new data as either a potential threat or benign. Unsupervised learning involves training algorithms on unlabeled data, where the model must identify patterns and anomalies without predefined categories. This technique is particularly useful for detecting unknown threats and anomalies that do not fit established patterns. For instance, unsupervised learning can help identify unusual network behavior that may indicate a new type of attack. Reinforcement learning involves training algorithms to make decisions based on feedback from their actions. In the context of threat detection, reinforcement learning can be used to continuously improve detection strategies by learning from past incidents and adjusting responses accordingly.

Anomaly Detection: This is a key application of this technology in threat detection. This technique involves identifying deviations from normal behavior that may indicate a security threat. By establishing a baseline of normal activity, these systems can flag unusual patterns that may suggest an attack. For example, in a network security context, an AI system might learn typical patterns of network traffic and identify deviations such as unusual data transfers or access attempts. These anomalies could indicate potential threats such as data exfiltration or unauthorized access.

Behavioral Analysis: Behavioral analysis involves monitoring and analyzing user and system behavior to detect signs of malicious activity. AI-driven systems can create profiles of normal behavior for users and devices, allowing them to detect deviations that may signal an attack. For instance, if an employee's account suddenly starts accessing sensitive data at odd hours or from unfamiliar locations, the security system can flag this behavior as suspicious. By focusing on behavioral patterns rather than specific attack signatures, these threat detection systems can identify threats that might otherwise go unnoticed.

Threat Intelligence Integration: Integrating threat intelligence with AI-driven systems enhances threat detection capabilities by providing context and actionable insights. Threat intelligence involves collecting and analyzing information about emerging threats, attack techniques, and adversary tactics. These security frameworks can incorporate threat intelligence feeds to enhance their detection capabilities. For example, if a new malware strain is identified and documented in threat intelligence sources, AI-driven systems can update their models to recognize the characteristics of this malware and improve detection accuracy.

Predictive Analytics for Threat Forecasting: AI and ML can leverage predictive analytics to anticipate potential security threats before they materialize. By analyzing historical attack patterns, emerging trends, and current threat landscapes, these systems can forecast potential future threats. This proactive approach allows organizations to prepare and strengthen their defenses against anticipated attack vectors, reducing the likelihood of successful breaches.

Automated Incident Response: This technology can automate incident response actions based on detected threats. For instance, when a threat is identified, the AI can automatically isolate affected systems, block malicious IP addresses, or apply predefined security rules to mitigate the threat. This automation speeds up the response process, reduces human error, and ensures a more consistent and timely reaction to security incidents.

Integration with Security Orchestration Platforms: This can enhance security orchestration platforms by providing context-aware insights and recommendations. These platforms integrate various security tools and processes to streamline operations and improve efficiency. AI-driven threat detection systems can feed valuable insights into these platforms, enabling more coordinated and effective security operations, including automated workflows and enhanced decision-making based on comprehensive threat intelligence.

The adoption of AI-driven threat detection systems offers several key benefits. For example, these systems can analyze vast amounts of data and identify patterns that might be missed by traditional methods. This leads to more accurate detection of both known and unknown threats, reducing the likelihood of false positives and false negatives. They can process data and detect threats in real-time, allowing for faster response and mitigation. Automated responses can be triggered based on detected threats, minimizing the impact of an attack and reducing the need for manual intervention.

These frameworks can also scale to handle large volumes of data and adapt to growing network environments. This scalability is particularly important in today's interconnected and data-rich environments, where traditional methods may struggle to keep up. AI systems can proactively identify potential threats and vulnerabilities before they are exploited. By analyzing patterns and behaviors, they can uncover hidden threats and provide early warnings, allowing organizations to address issues before they escalate.

Challenges and Considerations

While AI-driven threat detection offers significant advantages, there are also challenges and considerations to address:

Data Quality and Quantity: The effectiveness of AI and ML models relies on the quality and quantity of data they are trained on. Incomplete or biased data can lead to inaccurate detections and poor performance. Organizations must ensure they have access to high-quality data and continuously update their models to reflect changing threat landscapes.

Model Interpretability: The models can sometimes act as "black boxes," making it difficult to understand how they arrive at their conclusions. This lack of interpretability can be a challenge in security contexts, where understanding the rationale behind a detection is crucial for effective response and mitigation.

False Positives and False Negatives: While AI-driven systems aim to reduce false positives and false negatives, they are not immune to errors. Balancing detection accuracy with minimizing false alerts requires ongoing tuning and validation of models to ensure they perform effectively in real-world scenarios.

Adversarial Attacks: As the systems become more prevalent, they may become targets for adversarial attacks designed to deceive or mislead the models. Organizations must be aware of these risks and implement measures to safeguard their AI systems against manipulation.

Ethical and Privacy Concerns: The use of AI in threat detection raises ethical and privacy concerns, particularly regarding the collection and analysis of personal data. Organizations must navigate these concerns carefully, ensuring compliance with privacy regulations and maintaining transparency with users about data usage.

The future of this mechanism is promising, with ongoing advancements in AI and ML technologies expected to further enhance security capabilities. Emerging technologies such as quantum computing, advanced neural networks, and autonomous systems are likely to play a significant role in shaping the future of threat detection. It will continue to evolve, becoming more sophisticated and capable of addressing new and emerging threats. Collaboration between researchers, professionals, and industry stakeholders will be essential in driving innovation and ensuring that these systems are effective, ethical, and aligned with the needs of the security community.

In conclusion, AI-driven threat detection represents a significant advancement in the field of cybersecurity. By leveraging machine learning algorithms, anomaly detection, and behavioral analysis, organizations can enhance their ability to detect and respond to threats. While challenges remain, the benefits of the systems make them a valuable asset in the ongoing effort to safeguard digital assets and protect against cyber threats.

4. AUTOMATING INCIDENT RESPONSE

To survive in this era where cyber threats are increasingly sophisticated and pervasive, the speed and effectiveness of incident response are crucial for minimizing damage and maintaining operational integrity. Conventional incident response methods, often reliant on manual processes and human intervention, struggle to keep pace with the rapid evolution of threats. To address this challenge, organizations are turning to Artificial Intelligence (AI) to automate and enhance their incident response capabilities. We will be learning how AI-driven automation is revolutionizing incident response, exploring its benefits, technologies, and implementation strategies.

Understanding Incident Response

Incident response refers to the structured approach an organization takes to manage and mitigate the impact of a cybersecurity incident. This process involves several key stages: detection, analysis, containment, eradication, recovery, and post-incident review. The goal is to quickly identify and address threats to minimize disruption, reduce damage, and restore normal operations. Typically, incident response relies heavily on human analysts who monitor security alerts, investigate potential threats, and execute response actions. While skilled professionals are essential, the increasing volume and complexity of security incidents have made it challenging to manage these tasks manually. This is where AI-driven automation comes into play, offering a powerful solution to enhance the efficiency and effectiveness of incident response.

AI-driven automation transforms incident response by enabling faster, more accurate, and more scalable actions. There are key areas where this technology enhances incident response. These systems excel at processing vast amounts of data in real-time. Machine learning algorithms can analyze security logs, network traffic, and user behavior to detect anomalies and potential threats more quickly than traditional methods. For instance, the models can identify patterns indicative of an attack, such as unusual login attempts or data exfiltration activities. By automating the analysis of these signals, it helps ensure that threats are detected and assessed promptly. They are also employed for automated triage and prioritization. In a typical incident response scenario, security analysts must sift through numerous alerts to identify which ones warrant immediate attention. These frameworks can automate this triage process by classifying and prioritizing alerts based on their severity and potential impact. For example, an AI system might use historical data and threat intelligence to determine that a particular alert is likely to be a high-risk ransomware attack, while another is a low-priority phishing attempt. This prioritization enables analysts to focus on the most critical issues first.

Incident response playbooks outline predefined procedures for handling various types of security incidents. AI can automate the execution of these playbooks, adjusting the response actions based on real-time data and evolving circumstances. For example, if a security system detects a suspicious file, it can automatically follow a playbook that includes isolating the affected system, running a malware scan, and blocking the file's execution. This dynamic response ensures that appropriate actions are taken quickly and consistently. It can significantly speed up the containment and remediation of security incidents. Once a threat is identified, AI systems can execute predefined actions to contain the incident and prevent further damage. For instance, if a network breach is detected, it can automatically isolate the affected segment, revoke compromised credentials, and apply patches to vulnerable systems. These automated actions reduce the time between detection and mitigation, minimizing the impact of the attack.

They also have the potential to integrate threat intelligence feeds to provide context and actionable insights during an incident. By correlating real-time data with threat intelligence, this framework can offer recommendations on how to handle specific threats. For example, if an AI system identifies a new variant of malware, it can cross-reference this information with threat intelligence sources to provide details on the malware's behavior and suggest appropriate countermeasures. This integration helps ensure that responses are informed by the latest threat information. One of the significant advantages of AI in incident response is its ability to continuously learn and improve. Machine learning models can analyze past incidents to identify patterns and refine their detection and response capabilities. For instance, it might learn to recognize new tactics used by attackers based on historical data, improving its ability to detect similar threats in the future. This continuous learning process helps organizations stay ahead of evolving cyber threats.

Benefits and Disadvantages of AI-Driven Incident Response

The adoption of AI-driven automation in incident response offers several key benefits:

- Speed and Efficiency: AI systems can process and analyze data much faster than human analysts. This speed translates into quicker detection of threats and faster execution of response actions. By automating repetitive tasks, AI also frees up analysts to focus on more complex issues.

- Consistency and Accuracy: Automated systems execute predefined actions consistently and without error. This consistency reduces the risk of human mistakes and ensures that response procedures are followed accurately. The automation also minimizes the impact of alert fatigue, where analysts may overlook critical alerts due to overwhelming volumes.

- Scalability: As organizations grow and their networks become more complex, traditional incident response methods may struggle to keep up. AI-driven automation scales with the organization, handling large volumes of data and incidents without a proportional increase in human resources.

- Improved Resource Allocation: By automating routine tasks, it allows security teams to allocate their resources more effectively. Analysts can focus on higher-level tasks such as investigating complex threats and developing strategic defenses, while the structure handles routine monitoring and response actions.

- Enhanced Threat Detection: AI-driven systems can identify subtle patterns and anomalies that might be missed by traditional methods. This enhanced detection capability helps organizations uncover hidden threats and respond to them before they cause significant damage.

- Adaptive Threat Detection: They adapt to evolving threats by continuously learning from new data and attack patterns. Unlike static rule-based systems, AI can adjust its detection algorithms in real-time based on the latest threat intelligence and emerging attack techniques. This adaptability enhances the system's ability to identify and respond to novel and sophisticated threats more effectively.

- Cost Efficiency: Automating incident response with AI can lead to significant cost savings for organizations. By reducing the need for manual intervention and minimizing the time required to detect and respond to threats, they can lower operational costs associated with cybersecurity. Additionally, the efficiency gains can lead to reduced downtime and fewer resources spent on incident management, contributing to overall cost effectiveness.

While AI-driven automation offers numerous advantages, there are also challenges and considerations to address:

- Data Quality and Availability: The effectiveness of AI systems depends on the quality and quantity of data they are trained on. Inaccurate or incomplete data can lead to false positives or missed threats. Organizations must ensure they have access to high-quality data and continuously update their models to reflect changing threat landscapes.

- Integration with Existing Systems: Integrating the automation with existing security infrastructure can be complex. Organizations must ensure that systems are compatible with their current tools and processes, and that they can be seamlessly integrated into their incident response workflows.

- Model Interpretability: AI models can sometimes act as "black boxes," making it difficult to understand how they arrive at their conclusions. In a security context, understanding the rationale behind a decision is crucial for effective response and mitigation. Efforts should be made to enhance the interpretability of AI models and provide transparency in their decision-making processes.

- Ethical and Privacy Concerns: The use of the technology in incident response raises ethical and privacy concerns, particularly regarding the collection and analysis of personal data. Organizations must navigate these concerns carefully, ensuring compliance with privacy regulations and maintaining transparency with users about data usage.

- Adversarial Attacks on AI Systems: As they become more prevalent, they may become targets for adversarial attacks designed to deceive or manipulate the models. Organizations must implement measures to safeguard their AI systems against such attacks and ensure their resilience against adversarial tactics.

Implementing AI-Driven Incident Response

Beyond understanding and appreciating the use of AI in incident response, it is more imperative to take practical action towards utilizing it. To effectively implement the automation in incident response, organizations should consider the following steps:

1. **Define Objectives and Use Cases:** Clearly define the objectives and use cases for AI-driven incident response. Identify the specific areas where automation can add value, such as threat detection, response actions, or incident analysis. Establishing clear goals helps guide the implementation process and ensures alignment with organizational needs.

2. **Select Appropriate Technologies:** Choose the technologies and tools that align with your organization's requirements. Consider factors such as the types of threats you face, the volume of data you need to process, and the level of integration required with existing systems. Evaluate different AI solutions and select those that best meet your needs.

3. **Train and Validate Models:** Ensure that the models are trained on relevant and high-quality data. Continuously validate and update models to maintain their accuracy and effectiveness. Regularly assess the performance of the systems and make adjustments as needed to improve detection and response capabilities.

4. **Integrate with Existing Processes:** Integrate AI-driven automation with your existing incident response processes and tools. Ensure that the systems can seamlessly interact with your security infrastructure and that they complement rather than replace human

expertise. Establish workflows and protocols for how the actions will be handled and monitored.

5. Monitor and Evaluate Performance: Continuously monitor the performance of the incident response systems. Track key metrics such as detection accuracy, response times, and the number of incidents handled. Use this data to evaluate the effectiveness of AI automation and identify areas for improvement.

6. Address Ethical and Privacy Concerns: Ensure that the use of AI in incident response adheres to ethical standards and privacy regulations. Implement measures to protect personal data and maintain transparency with stakeholders about how data is collected and used. Address any ethical concerns proactively to build trust and ensure compliance.

The technology is poised to bring even more advancements and capabilities. As AI trends continue to evolve, we can expect to see further improvements in automation, accuracy, and integration. Emerging trends such as AI-powered threat intelligence, autonomous response systems, and advanced behavioral analytics will play a significant role in shaping the future of incident response. This tool represents a transformative approach to incident response, offering speed, accuracy, and scalability in managing cybersecurity incidents.

5. BEHAVIORAL ANALYSIS AND ANOMALY DETECTION

Advanced techniques like behavioral analysis and anomaly detection have emerged as critical tools in ensuring cyber defense. These methods leverage Artificial Intelligence (AI) to enhance the identification of threats, moving beyond static and signature-based approaches to provide more nuanced and adaptable security solutions. This chapter delves into how AI-driven behavioral analysis and anomaly detection are transforming threat identification, exploring their methodologies, real-world applications, and future directions.

What is Behavioral Analysis and Anomaly Detection

Behavioral Analysis involves monitoring and evaluating the behavior of users, systems, and network activities to detect deviations from established norms. By focusing on behavior rather than known threat signatures, this approach can identify previously unknown or evolving threats that do not match traditional attack patterns. Anomaly Detection, on the other hand, refers to identifying patterns in data that deviate from the expected or normal behavior. It relies on statistical models and machine learning algorithms to flag unusual activities that may indicate potential security incidents. Both techniques are crucial for recognizing threats that bypass conventional detection methods.

AI enhances behavioral analysis through machine learning and data analytics, enabling systems to learn from and adapt to complex patterns of behavior. Here's how it drives this process:

Pattern Recognition and Learning: AI-driven behavioral analysis systems utilize machine learning algorithms to recognize and learn patterns of normal behavior across various entities, including users, devices, and applications. For instance, algorithms can analyze login times, data access patterns, and user interactions to build a profile of typical behavior.

Once a baseline of normal behavior is established, the system continuously monitors for deviations. For example, if an employee's account suddenly starts accessing sensitive data or shows login attempts from unfamiliar locations, the AI can flag these activities as anomalies. This ability to recognize subtle changes in behavior helps detect insider threats, compromised accounts, and other potential security incidents.

Behavioral Profiling and Anomaly Detection: These systems create detailed behavioral profiles for users and entities by analyzing historical data and interactions. These profiles include a range of activities such as typical login times, frequency of data access, and usual communication patterns. When new activities deviate from these profiles, AI algorithms can identify potential threats. For example, if a user who typically accesses a particular set of files suddenly tries to access an extensive list of confidential documents, the system can flag this behavior as suspicious. AI's capacity to handle large volumes of data and identify subtle deviations makes it highly effective for detecting complex threats that might elude traditional methods.

Adaptive Learning and Continuous Improvement: They continuously learn from new data, allowing them to adapt to evolving behaviors and attack techniques. As attackers modify their tactics, AI models can update their understanding of normal behavior and adjust their detection algorithms accordingly. This adaptive learning process is crucial for maintaining effective threat detection. For instance, if an attacker starts using new methods to blend in with normal user behavior, the AI system can learn these new patterns and refine its detection capabilities. This continuous improvement helps keep pace with emerging threats and ensures that the system remains effective over time.

Enhanced Insider Threat Detection: It is particularly effective at identifying insider threats by monitoring deviations in user behavior. For example, if an employee who typically follows standard procedures suddenly starts accessing files or systems outside their usual scope of work, AI systems can flag this behavior as potentially suspicious. By analyzing patterns such as unusual data access times, changes in file retrieval frequency, or deviations from normal communication channels, it can help detect malicious activities or policy violations that might indicate an insider threat. This capability is crucial for protecting sensitive information and maintaining organizational security.

Anomaly Correlation Across Multiple Data Sources: They can correlate anomalies detected across various data sources to provide a more comprehensive view of potential threats. For instance, an AI-driven system might analyze user behavior, network traffic, and system logs to identify patterns that suggest a coordinated attack or sophisticated threat. By integrating and cross-referencing data from multiple sources, it can enhance the accuracy of anomaly detection and provide a more nuanced understanding of complex security incidents.

This multi-faceted approach helps in identifying complex threats that involve multiple vectors or stages, improving overall detection and response strategies.

Anomaly detection powered by AI focuses on identifying unusual patterns in large datasets, often utilizing machine learning and statistical analysis techniques. Here's how AI enhances anomaly detection:

Statistical and Machine Learning Models: AI-driven anomaly detection uses various statistical and machine learning models to analyze data and identify deviations from normal patterns. Common techniques include statistical methods and machine learning algorithms. Statistical models such as z-scores and Gaussian distributions are used to identify outliers in data. For example, if network traffic deviates significantly from the historical average, it may be flagged as an anomaly. Machine learning models such as clustering algorithms (e.g., k-means) and classification algorithms (e.g., decision trees) can identify anomalies by analyzing patterns in data. For instance, unsupervised learning algorithms can detect unusual network behaviors without prior knowledge of specific attack patterns.

Real-Time Monitoring and Detection: They can process and analyze large volumes of data in real-time, enabling rapid detection of anomalies. Real-time monitoring is essential for identifying and responding to threats before they cause significant damage. For example, AI-driven systems can analyze network traffic, user activities, and system logs to detect anomalies as they occur, allowing for timely intervention.

Context-Aware Anomaly Detection: AI-driven anomaly detection can incorporate contextual information to improve accuracy. Context-aware systems analyze not only the data but also the context in which it occurs. For instance, if an anomaly is detected in network traffic, the system may consider factors such as the time of day, user roles, and recent activities to determine whether the anomaly is a potential threat. By integrating contextual information, these systems can reduce false positives and enhance the relevance of detected anomalies. This contextual awareness helps ensure that the alerts generated are actionable and meaningful.

Predictive Analysis for Proactive Threat Mitigation: They go beyond merely identifying unusual patterns by using predictive analysis to anticipate potential threats before they fully materialize. By examining historical data and recognizing trends or emerging patterns, AI systems can forecast future anomalies that may indicate developing threats. For example, if an AI model detects a gradual increase in unusual login attempts or data access activities over time, it can predict a higher likelihood of a security breach or attack. This predictive capability allows organizations to take preemptive measures, such as tightening access controls or increasing monitoring, to mitigate potential risks before they escalate.

Dynamic Threshold Adjustment: AI systems can dynamically adjust the thresholds for anomaly detection based on evolving data patterns and contextual information. Unlike static threshold systems that rely on predefined limits, they can modify detection parameters in real-time according to changes in user behavior, network traffic, or system performance. For instance, if a model detects a shift in normal user activity during a seasonal event or a major organizational change, it can recalibrate its thresholds to maintain accurate detection capabilities. This dynamic adjustment helps prevent both false positives and false negatives, ensuring that the system remains sensitive to relevant anomalies while minimizing unnecessary alerts.

Real-World Applications

The application of AI-driven behavioral analysis and anomaly detection is widespread, with significant impacts across various industries. Here are some real-world examples:

Financial Sector: In the financial sector, AI-driven behavioral analysis is used to detect fraudulent transactions and account compromises. For instance, banks utilize machine learning models to analyze transaction patterns and identify anomalies such as unusual spending behaviors or transactions from unfamiliar locations. These systems help prevent fraud and secure sensitive financial data.

Healthcare: It is employed to identify irregularities in patient data and medical records. For example, AI systems can monitor electronic health records (EHRs) for anomalies that may indicate fraudulent activities or data breaches. Behavioral analysis can also be used to detect unusual access patterns to patient information, ensuring compliance with privacy regulations.

E-Commerce: E-commerce platforms use AI-driven behavioral analysis to enhance customer security and prevent fraudulent activities. For instance, online retailers analyze user behavior to detect anomalies such as suspicious login attempts, irregular purchasing patterns, or account takeovers. By identifying these anomalies, e-commerce platforms can protect customer accounts and prevent fraudulent transactions.

Enterprise IT Security: These environments leverage AI-driven behavioral analysis and anomaly detection to safeguard against insider threats and data breaches. For example, organizations monitor employee activities to identify deviations from normal behavior, such as accessing sensitive data without authorization or exhibiting unusual network behaviors. AI systems can also detect anomalies in system logs and network traffic to identify potential security incidents.

To effectively implement AI-driven behavioral analysis and anomaly detection, organizations should begin by focusing on robust data collection and preparation. This involves gathering comprehensive data from various sources, such as user activities, network traffic, and system logs, and ensuring it is clean, normalized, and relevant. High-quality data is crucial for training accurate AI models, so attention to data integrity and completeness is essential. Once data is prepared, selecting and training appropriate machine learning models is the next step. Organizations should evaluate different algorithms and methodologies based on their specific needs and data characteristics to ensure effective anomaly detection.

Integration with existing security infrastructure is another critical component. These systems should complement rather than replace current security tools and workflows, requiring careful planning to ensure seamless interaction. Continuous monitoring and evaluation of AI systems are necessary to maintain their effectiveness, involving regular assessments of model performance and adjustments based on evolving threats. Collaboration among data scientists, cybersecurity experts, and domain specialists will enhance the implementation process, ensuring that these systems are tailored to organizational requirements and capable of providing actionable insights.

AI-driven behavioral analysis and anomaly detection offer several compelling advantages that enhance threat detection and security management. One of the primary benefits is the ability to identify sophisticated and novel threats that traditional methods might miss. By focusing on behavioral patterns rather than known signatures, they can detect unusual activities indicative of advanced persistent threats or insider attacks, which are often not recognized by conventional security measures. These systems excel in processing vast amounts of data in real-time, allowing for rapid detection and response. This speed is critical in mitigating potential damage and preventing breaches before they escalate. Moreover, AI's adaptive learning capabilities enable continuous improvement in threat detection. As the models learn from new data and evolving attack techniques, they refine their detection algorithms, ensuring they stay effective against emerging threats. The automation of routine tasks, such as monitoring and alerting, also frees up human analysts to focus on more complex issues, optimizing resource allocation and improving overall efficiency. Additionally, this technology can integrate contextual information to enhance the accuracy of anomaly detection, reducing false positives and ensuring that alerts are actionable.

Despite their advantages, AI-driven behavioral analysis and anomaly detection systems come with certain drawbacks. One significant challenge is the dependency on the quality and quantity of data used for training AI models. Inaccurate or incomplete data can lead to false positives or missed threats, compromising the effectiveness of the system. Additionally, the models can sometimes act as "black boxes," making it difficult to understand the rationale behind their decisions. This lack of transparency can hinder trust in the system and complicate the interpretation of detected anomalies. The integration of AI systems with existing security infrastructure can also be complex and resource-intensive. Ensuring compatibility and seamless interaction with other tools and processes requires careful planning and implementation. Furthermore, ethical and privacy concerns arise with the use of AI in monitoring and analyzing user behavior. Organizations must navigate issues related to data privacy, consent, and the responsible use of AI technologies to maintain compliance and build trust. Lastly, AI-driven systems can be vulnerable to adversarial attacks designed to manipulate or deceive the models, highlighting the need for robust safeguards to protect against such threats.

Looking ahead, the future of behavioral analysis and anomaly detection is likely to be shaped by several transformative trends. A significant development is the push towards enhancing the explainability and interpretability of these models. As systems become more complex, there is a growing need to make their decision-making processes transparent and comprehensible. This focus will help organizations understand the rationale behind detected anomalies, build trust in the technology, and ensure that the insights provided are actionable and reliable. Additionally, integrating advanced threat intelligence sources with detection capabilities will offer a more comprehensive view of the threat landscape, improving contextual awareness and overall effectiveness.

Future advancements also point towards the evolution of adaptive and self-learning models. These technologies will autonomously refine their detection algorithms based on new data and evolving attack techniques, maintaining their effectiveness against increasingly sophisticated threats. Collaboration between automated systems and human analysts will enhance security operations, with machines handling routine tasks and providing insights while humans focus on strategic decision-making. Moreover, addressing ethical and privacy concerns will become more critical, as responsible use and compliance with privacy regulations will be essential for maintaining trust and protecting sensitive information.

Behavioral analysis and anomaly detection powered by AI represent significant advancements in the field of cybersecurity. By leveraging machine learning and statistical techniques, organizations can identify threats with greater accuracy and efficiency, moving beyond traditional signature-based methods. The integration of AI into threat detection processes offers enhanced capabilities for recognizing complex and evolving threats, improving security posture, and protecting critical assets. By embracing these advancements and addressing associated challenges, organizations can stay ahead of emerging threats and ensure a robust defense against an increasingly dynamic cyber threat landscape.

6. PREDICTIVE ANALYTICS IN CYBERSECURITY

The growing complexity of attacks and the sheer volume of data necessitate a shift towards more proactive strategies. Predictive analytics, powered by artificial intelligence (AI), offers a promising avenue for anticipating and mitigating cyber threats before they manifest. This chapter delves into how predictive analytics works in cybersecurity, its methodologies, applications, benefits, and challenges.

Understanding Predictive Analytics

Predictive analytics refers to the use of statistical techniques, machine learning, and AI to analyze historical data and make forecasts about future events. This means leveraging data to predict potential threats, identify vulnerabilities, and anticipate attack vectors.

Traditionally, security systems relied heavily on reactive measures such as patching vulnerabilities after they were exploited and responding to security incidents as they occurred. The advent of predictive analytics marks a shift towards a more proactive approach, where patterns and trends are analyzed to foresee potential threats.

AI technology has played a significant role in enhancing the current stance and operations of predictive analytics particularly in security of digital infrastructure. Some of these are:

Machine Learning (ML): Machine learning algorithms analyze large datasets to identify patterns and anomalies that might indicate a threat. Techniques like supervised learning, unsupervised learning, and reinforcement learning are utilized.

Deep Learning: A subset of machine learning that uses neural networks with multiple layers to analyze complex data patterns. Deep learning can be particularly effective in detecting sophisticated threats that might evade traditional methods.

Natural Language Processing (NLP): NLP helps in analyzing textual data from various sources, such as threat intelligence feeds, social media, and dark web forums, to identify emerging threats and vulnerabilities.

This technology also enhances predictive analytics by improving the accuracy of predictions and reducing the time required to identify potential threats. Machine learning models can process vast amounts of data in real-time, enabling quicker responses and more informed decision-making.

Predictive analytics methodologies in cybersecurity involve using statistical techniques and machine learning algorithms to analyze historical and real-time data to forecast potential threats and vulnerabilities. These methodologies include anomaly detection, classification, and regression analysis to identify patterns and predict future attack behaviors.

Data Collection and Integration: Effective predictive analytics begins with comprehensive data collection. This includes data from network logs, user behavior, threat intelligence feeds, and more. Integrating data from various sources ensures a holistic view of the security landscape.

Feature Engineering: This involves selecting and transforming raw data into meaningful features that can improve the performance of predictive models. This might involve creating new features from existing data or selecting the most relevant features for analysis.

Model Selection and Training: This encompass anomaly detection, classification and regression analysis. In anomaly detection, models are trained to identify deviations from normal behavior, which might indicate a security threat. Techniques include clustering and statistical methods. Classification models categorize data into predefined classes, such as benign or malicious. Common algorithms include decision trees, support vector machines, and neural networks. Regression models predict future events based on historical data. In this setting, regression might be used to estimate the likelihood of an attack based on past incidents.

Evaluation and Validation: Models need to be evaluated for accuracy, precision, recall, and other performance metrics. Validation techniques such as cross-validation and hold-out validation help ensure that models generalize well to new data.

Applications of Predictive Analytics in Cybersecurity

Here, we examine briefly how this concept can be practically applied and real-world case studies to aid us grasp it more effectively.

- Threat Intelligence: Predictive analytics can enhance threat intelligence by analyzing data from various sources to identify emerging threats. By recognizing patterns and trends, organizations can anticipate attacks and implement preventive measures.

- Behavior Analysis: Monitoring user behavior and network traffic using predictive models helps in detecting anomalies that might indicate a breach. For example, unusual login patterns or irregular data access can trigger alerts for further investigation.

- Vulnerability Management: Predictive analytics can help in prioritizing vulnerabilities based on the likelihood of exploitation. By analyzing historical attack data and current threat landscapes, organizations can focus on addressing the most critical vulnerabilities.

- Incident Response: During an active attack, predictive models can assist in identifying the attacker's tactics, techniques, and procedures (TTPs). This information helps in crafting a more effective response and mitigating the attack more efficiently.

- Fraud Detection: In financial institutions and other sectors, predictive analytics can be used to detect fraudulent transactions by analyzing patterns and anomalies in transaction data.

Predictive analytics offers significant advantages by enabling a proactive approach to threat management. Leveraging AI and machine learning, it enhances threat detection accuracy and efficiency by analyzing vast amounts of data to identify patterns and anomalies indicative of potential attacks. This early detection allows organizations to mitigate threats before they escalate, optimizing resource allocation and reducing response times. Predictive analytics also improves overall security posture by enabling better-informed decision-making and prioritization of vulnerabilities based on their likelihood of exploitation.

Despite its benefits, its reliance on large volumes of data raises concerns about data privacy and security, necessitating stringent measures to protect sensitive information. Additionally, predictive models can suffer from limitations such as false positives and false negatives, potentially leading to incorrect threat assessments or missed attacks. The rapidly evolving nature of cyber threats requires continuous model updates and maintenance, which can be resource-intensive. Integrating predictive analytics with existing security infrastructure may also pose technical and operational challenges, requiring significant adjustments and investment.

Real-World Case Studies and Applications

Case Study 1: Darktrace's Autonomous Response

Background: Darktrace, a prominent cybersecurity firm with its headquarters in Cambridge, London, employs AI-driven predictive analytics to detect and respond to cyber threats in real-time. The company's technology, known as the Enterprise Immune System, uses machine learning to model the behavior of every user and device within a network.

Application: Darktrace's system learns what constitutes normal behavior for each user and device. By continuously analyzing network traffic and behavior, it can identify deviations from the norm that may indicate a potential threat. For instance, if an employee's account starts downloading unusual amounts of data or accessing restricted areas of the network, Darktrace's system will flag this as an anomaly.

Impact: It has successfully prevented numerous attacks by detecting threats before they could cause significant damage. The autonomous response capability allows the system to take immediate action, such as isolating a compromised device or blocking suspicious activities, thereby minimizing the impact of potential breaches.

Case Study 2: IBM's QRadar Security Intelligence Platform

Background: IBM QRadar is a comprehensive security information and event management (SIEM) platform that integrates predictive analytics to enhance threat detection and response.

Application: It uses machine learning algorithms to analyze security data from various sources, including network logs, endpoint data, and threat intelligence feeds. The platform employs advanced analytics to correlate data points and identify patterns indicative of potential threats. For example, it can detect sophisticated multi-stage attacks by analyzing the sequence of events and their correlation across different systems.

Impact: Organizations using QRadar have reported improved threat detection capabilities and faster incident response times. By leveraging predictive analytics, QRadar helps security teams prioritize threats and allocate resources more effectively, thereby enhancing overall security posture.

Case Study 3: Microsoft Azure Sentinel

Background: Microsoft Azure Sentinel is a cloud-native SIEM solution that uses AI and machine learning to provide advanced threat detection and response capabilities.

Application: Azure Sentinel employs predictive analytics to analyze vast amounts of security data and detect potential threats. It uses built-in machine learning models to identify anomalies and potential attacks. For instance, it can detect unusual login activities, such as failed login attempts from geographically disparate locations, which may indicate a compromised account.

Impact: Its predictive capabilities have enabled organizations to identify and respond to threats more quickly and accurately. Its integration with other Microsoft security tools and third-party solutions enhances its effectiveness, providing a comprehensive security solution.

Case Study 4: Palo Alto Networks Cortex XDR

Background: Palo Alto Networks Cortex XDR (Extended Detection and Response) leverages predictive analytics to provide a unified approach to threat detection and response across endpoints, networks, and clouds.

Application: The system uses advanced machine learning algorithms to analyze data from multiple sources, including endpoint activity, network traffic, and cloud services. The platform correlates data to detect complex attack patterns and provide actionable insights.

For example, it can identify a coordinated attack that spans multiple attack vectors by analyzing patterns across different data sources.

Impact: Cortex XDR's predictive analytics capabilities have significantly improved the ability to detect and respond to advanced threats. By providing a unified view of threats and automating response actions, it helps organizations reduce the time to detect and mitigate attacks.

Case Study 5: FireEye's Helix Security Platform

Background: FireEye's Helix Security Platform integrates predictive analytics with threat intelligence to enhance cybersecurity operations.

Application: Helix uses machine learning and AI to analyze security data and predict potential threats. It correlates data from various sources, including threat intelligence feeds, network logs, and endpoint data. For instance, it can predict the likelihood of an attack based on emerging threat trends and historical data, enabling organizations to take proactive measures.

Impact: The integration of predictive analytics in Helix has enhanced threat detection and response capabilities. Organizations have been able to anticipate and prevent attacks more effectively, leveraging predictive insights to prioritize security measures and allocate resources more efficiently.

Future trends we expect to see are poised to leverage advancements in AI and machine learning to enhance threat detection and response. As technologies like quantum computing and advanced neural networks evolve, they promise to improve the accuracy and speed of predictive models, enabling even more sophisticated threat forecasting and mitigation strategies. Increased automation will also play a significant role, with predictive analytics driving automated threat detection and response systems that can rapidly address emerging threats with minimal human intervention.

Another trend is the growing emphasis on collaboration and data sharing among organizations to strengthen predictive analytics capabilities. By pooling threat intelligence and sharing insights, organizations can gain a more comprehensive view of the threat landscape, improving the effectiveness of predictive models. Additionally, as predictive analytics becomes more integral to cybersecurity, addressing ethical and regulatory considerations will be crucial to ensure responsible use of AI-driven solutions, protecting data privacy and maintaining transparency.

Predictive analytics, powered by AI, represents a significant advancement in improving security frameworks. By leveraging historical data and sophisticated algorithms, organizations can anticipate and mitigate threats more effectively than ever before. While challenges remain, the benefits of predictive analytics such as proactive threat management, enhanced accuracy, and improved efficiency make it a valuable tool to have in one's arsenal. As technology continues to evolve, predictive analytics will play an increasingly central role in safeguarding digital environments from ever-evolving cyber threats.

7. THE ROLE OF AI IN IDENTIFYING AND MITIGATING ZERO- DAY EXPLOITS

Zero-day exploits represent a particularly insidious threat in the sphere of cybersecurity. These vulnerabilities are unknown to software vendors and security experts at the time they are exploited, leaving systems and networks exposed to potentially catastrophic attacks. The traditional methods of detecting and mitigating these exploits are often insufficient, given the stealthy nature of zero-day threats. However, artificial intelligence (AI) offers a transformative approach to addressing this challenge. We will explore how AI can enhance the identification and mitigation of zero-day exploits, detailing methodologies, real-world applications, benefits, and future trends.

What is Zero-Day Exploits

A zero-day exploit targets a previously unknown vulnerability in software or hardware that has not yet been patched or addressed by the vendor. The term "zero-day" refers to the fact that the exploit is used before the vendor has had any "days" to fix the flaw. Key characteristics include unknown vulnerability, high risk and urgency. In unknown vulnerability, the flaw is not known to the vendor or security community. High risk refers to exploits which can cause significant damage, such as data breaches or system compromises. Finally, urgency means rapid detection and response are crucial due to the exploit's covert nature.

Real-world examples, such as the Stuxnet worm or the Equation Group's exploits, illustrate the potential damage zero-day attacks can inflict. The impact ranges from operational disruption to data loss, highlighting the need for advanced detection and mitigation strategies.

Groups typically targeted by zero-day exploits include high-value entities such as government agencies, financial institutions, technology companies, and critical infrastructure providers. These organizations are attractive targets due to their access to sensitive information, substantial financial resources, or crucial operational systems. For instance, financial institutions hold valuable personal and financial data, while critical infrastructure providers manage systems vital for public safety and national security. Zero-day exploits against these groups can lead to significant data breaches, operational disruptions, or even national security threats, making them high-priority targets for attackers.

Mitigating this vulnerability is essential for all because the repercussions of successful attacks can extend beyond individual organizations to impact society at large. When critical infrastructure or financial systems are compromised, it can disrupt public services, erode trust in financial systems, and even endanger lives. Furthermore, the interconnected nature of modern digital ecosystems means that vulnerabilities in one sector can have cascading effects across others. Effective mitigation not only protects individual organizations but also safeguards the broader digital infrastructure, ensuring stability, security, and resilience in our increasingly interconnected world.

These are several AI technologies in zero-day exploit detection.

Machine Learning (ML) and Pattern Recognition: Machine learning plays a pivotal role in detecting zero-day exploits by recognizing patterns and anomalies in data that may indicate a new exploit. Key approaches include anomaly detection where ML models analyze baseline behaviors and detect deviations that could signal an exploit. A second approach is behavioral analysis. Here, models observe the behavior of software and users to identify suspicious activities that might be indicative of a zero-day exploit.

Deep Learning and Neural Networks: Deep learning enhances zero-day exploit detection by leveraging neural networks to analyze complex patterns and relationships in data. Techniques include feature extraction and advanced classification. In feature extraction, neural networks identify and extract relevant features from vast datasets to detect subtle signs of exploitation. For advanced classification, deep learning models classify new threats based on learned patterns from previous data, improving the detection of previously unknown exploits.

Natural Language Processing (NLP): This can be utilized to analyze textual data from threat intelligence feeds, security forums, and other sources. By processing and understanding unstructured data, AI can uncover emerging threats and vulnerabilities related to zero-day exploits.

Predictive Modeling Techniques: AI can be instrumental in forecasting future zero-day exploits by analyzing trends and patterns in historical attack data. Predictive modeling techniques, such as time series analysis and trend forecasting, use historical data to identify emerging threat patterns and predict potential future vulnerabilities. By integrating threat intelligence and historical exploit data, these models can anticipate the development of new attack vectors and provide early warnings.

Threat Landscape Analysis: These systems can continuously monitor and analyze the evolving threat landscape by aggregating data from multiple sources, including security forums, research papers, and dark web intelligence. Machine learning algorithms can identify correlations and trends that might indicate the emergence of new zero-day threats. For example, increasing discussions about specific software vulnerabilities or novel attack techniques in threat intelligence feeds can signal potential future exploits.

AI-Driven Simulation Models: Scenario planning and simulation are crucial for preparing for potential zero-day exploits. AI-driven simulation models can recreate various attack scenarios based on predicted vulnerabilities and threat patterns. By simulating potential zero-day exploits in a controlled environment, organizations can assess the impact of different attack vectors and develop effective response strategies.

Stress Testing Security Measures: AI can be used to conduct stress tests on existing security measures to evaluate their effectiveness against anticipated zero-day exploits. By simulating attacks and assessing the system's response, organizations can identify weaknesses and make necessary adjustments to their defenses. This proactive approach helps ensure that security measures are robust and capable of handling emerging threats.

Integrating AI with Threat Intelligence Platforms: They can aid in enhancing threat intelligence platforms by automating the analysis of vast amounts of threat data. Machine learning algorithms can sift through threat intelligence feeds, malware samples, and attack reports to identify emerging trends and potential zero-day vulnerabilities. This integration enables security teams to stay ahead of evolving threats and make informed decisions about their security posture.

Predictive Threat Intelligence: Predictive threat intelligence uses AI to provide actionable insights into future threats. By analyzing historical data and current threat trends, AI can generate predictions about potential zero-day exploits and emerging attack techniques. This proactive intelligence allows organizations to implement preventive measures and reduce the likelihood of successful attacks.

Collaborative AI Research and Development: Collaborative efforts in AI research and development can improve the ability to predict and address future zero-day exploits. Partnerships between academia, industry, and government agencies can drive innovation and share knowledge about emerging threats and vulnerabilities. Joint research initiatives can enhance AI models and provide more accurate predictions of future zero-day exploits.

Industry-Wide Threat Intelligence Sharing: Sharing threat intelligence across industries can enhance the ability to anticipate future zero-day exploits. AI-driven platforms that facilitate information sharing enable organizations to access a broader range of data and insights. By collaborating with peers and industry groups, organizations can gain a more comprehensive understanding of emerging threats and develop more effective defense strategies.

AI-Based Mitigation Strategies for Zero-Day Exploits and Case Studies

AI-based mitigation strategies are revolutionizing how organizations address zero-day exploits by enhancing response capabilities and automating key processes. Automated patch management is a significant advancement, where predictive models analyze historical data and threat intelligence to identify which vulnerabilities are most likely to be targeted. This allows for the prioritization and deployment of patches more effectively, reducing the window of opportunity for attackers. Additionally, automated systems ensure timely updates and minimize human error, which is crucial for maintaining robust defenses against emerging threats.

Behavioral-based prevention has also seen improvements through continuous monitoring and analysis of software and network activities. By detecting anomalies indicative of zero-day exploits, these systems enable real-time blocking of exploit attempts and adjust defenses dynamically as new threats emerge. Integrating threat intelligence with these systems further strengthens mitigation efforts by providing real-time insights and contextual awareness. This comprehensive approach allows for rapid detection, analysis, and response, significantly enhancing an organization's ability to protect against and mitigate zero-day exploits effectively.

Case Studies: AI in Action Against Zero-Day Exploits

Case Study 1: Google Project Zero

Background: Google's Project Zero is a research team focused on discovering and reporting zero-day vulnerabilities. The team utilizes AI and machine learning to identify and analyze these vulnerabilities.

Application: Project Zero employs AI to sift through vast amounts of code and data, using machine learning models to detect potential vulnerabilities. The team also analyzes exploit behavior to understand and mitigate new threats.

Impact: It has successfully identified numerous zero-day vulnerabilities and contributed to the development of timely patches. AI's role in automating and accelerating the discovery process has been crucial in addressing these high-risk threats.

Case Study 2: CrowdStrike Falcon

Background: CrowdStrike Falcon is a cybersecurity platform that leverages AI to provide endpoint protection and threat intelligence.

Application: It uses machine learning and behavioral analysis to detect zero-day exploits by monitoring endpoint activity and identifying suspicious behaviors. The platform's AI-driven approach allows for rapid detection and response to novel threats.

Impact: CrowdStrike Falcon has demonstrated the effectiveness of AI in mitigating zero-day exploits by providing real-time protection and reducing the time to detect and respond to emerging threats.

Case Study 3: Darktrace Enterprise Immune System

Background: Darktrace's Enterprise Immune System employs AI to model normal behavior within a network and detect anomalies that could indicate zero-day exploits.

Application: The system uses unsupervised machine learning to establish a baseline of normal network behavior and identify deviations that may suggest an exploit. It autonomously responds to these anomalies by taking preventive actions.

Impact: Darktrace's AI-driven approach has proven effective in identifying and mitigating zero-day exploits by leveraging behavioral analysis and automated responses, enhancing overall network security.

The advantages of using AI in identifying and mitigating zero-day exploits are substantial. AI enhances threat detection capabilities by analyzing vast amounts of data and recognizing patterns that might indicate previously unknown vulnerabilities. Machine learning models and advanced algorithms can detect subtle anomalies and sophisticated attack behaviors that traditional methods might miss, allowing for earlier and more accurate identification of potential threats. Additionally, AI-driven systems automate many aspects of threat response, such as patch management and behavioral analysis, which significantly speeds up the detection and mitigation processes. This automation reduces the time window during which zero-day exploits can be exploited, thus minimizing potential damage. Furthermore, AI systems continuously learn and adapt, improving their ability to detect and respond to new threats as they evolve, which helps maintain a proactive security posture.

However, the use of AI in this context is not without its challenges. One significant disadvantage is the risk of false positives and false negatives, where AI models might incorrectly flag benign activities as threats or fail to identify actual exploits. This can lead to unnecessary disruptions or missed vulnerabilities. Data privacy and security concerns also arise, as the collection and analysis of large datasets can pose risks if not managed properly. Additionally, AI systems require ongoing updates and maintenance to remain effective against new attack vectors, which can be resource-intensive. Integrating AI with existing cybersecurity infrastructure may present technical and operational challenges, requiring significant adjustments and investments. Lastly, the evolving nature of zero-day exploits means that AI models must continually adapt, which can be challenging given the rapid pace of technological change and emerging threats.

Artificial intelligence represents a powerful tool in the fight against zero-day exploits, offering enhanced detection, faster response, and continuous adaptation to emerging threats. While challenges such as false positives, data privacy, and integration remain, the benefits of AI in identifying and mitigating zero-day vulnerabilities are substantial.

8. AI POWERED THREAT INTELLIGENCE

Threat intelligence is crucial for preemptively addressing risks before they escalate into major incidents. Traditional methods of threat intelligence, which often depend on manual processes and outdated data sources, are increasingly inadequate in the face of a constantly evolving threat landscape. Artificial intelligence (AI) presents a game-changing opportunity by significantly improving threat intelligence through sophisticated data aggregation and analysis capabilities. This chapter will examine how AI-driven threat intelligence can transform cybersecurity practices by delivering more precise, timely, and actionable insights. We will explore the underlying mechanisms of AI-enhanced threat intelligence, its diverse applications, the advantages it offers, the challenges it faces, and the directions it may take in the future.

Threat intelligence involves the collection, analysis, and dissemination of information about current and emerging threats to an organization's information systems. This intelligence helps organizations understand potential risks, anticipate attacks, and implement effective defense strategies. It encompasses various types of data, including indicators of compromise (IOCs), tactics, techniques, and procedures (TTPs) used by adversaries, and contextual information about threat actors. Effective threat intelligence is crucial for proactive security measures, helping organizations stay ahead of threats and mitigate risks before they materialize.

Conventional methods often rely on manual processes and static data sources. Analysts collect data from various sources, such as threat feeds, security reports, and incident logs, and manually analyze this information to identify potential threats. While these methods provide valuable insights, they are often time-consuming, labor-intensive, and may not scale effectively with the increasing volume of threat data. Additionally, traditional approaches may struggle to detect emerging threats quickly enough due to their reliance on historical data and reactive analysis.

The Role and Application of AI in Threat Intelligence

Here are some ways this technology plays a part in advancing threat intelligence.

Data Aggregation with AI: AI enhances threat intelligence by automating and accelerating the aggregation of data from diverse sources. AI systems can ingest vast amounts of structured and unstructured data, including threat feeds, social media, dark web sources, and internal security logs. Natural language processing (NLP) and machine learning algorithms enable AI to process and interpret this data, identifying relevant threat indicators and patterns. By aggregating data from multiple sources, AI provides a comprehensive view of the threat landscape, allowing for more accurate and timely insights.

Advanced Analysis Techniques: AI-driven analysis techniques offer significant improvements over traditional methods. Machine learning algorithms, such as clustering, classification, and anomaly detection, analyze aggregated data to identify patterns and anomalies that may indicate potential threats. For example, clustering algorithms group similar threat data, helping analysts recognize trends and emerging threats. Classification algorithms categorize threats based on their characteristics, while anomaly detection identifies deviations from normal behavior that could signal new attack vectors. These advanced techniques enable more effective identification and prioritization of threats.

Predictive Analytics: Predictive analytics, powered by this technology, enhances threat intelligence by forecasting potential future threats based on historical data and emerging trends. Machine learning models analyze historical attack data, threat feeds, and other relevant information to predict the likelihood of specific threats occurring. Predictive analytics can help organizations anticipate new attack vectors, identify vulnerable areas, and implement proactive defenses. For example, predictive models may indicate an increased risk of ransomware attacks targeting a particular industry, allowing organizations to strengthen their defenses in advance.

Various methods of its application include:

Real-Time Threat Detection: AI-powered threat intelligence systems offer real-time threat detection capabilities by continuously monitoring and analyzing data from various sources. Machine learning algorithms detect and respond to emerging threats by analyzing patterns, behaviors, and anomalies in real-time. For example, these systems can identify and block malicious activities as they occur, providing immediate protection against zero-day exploits and other advanced threats. Real-time threat detection enables organizations to respond quickly and effectively, minimizing the impact of potential attacks.

Incident Response and Forensics: It enhances incident response and forensics by providing automated analysis and actionable insights. During a security incident, AI systems can analyze large volumes of data to identify the root cause, scope, and impact of the attack. Machine learning algorithms can help trace the attack's path, identify affected systems, and determine the techniques used by the adversary. This information aids in a more efficient and accurate response, helping organizations contain and remediate the incident effectively. Additionally, it can assist in post-incident forensics by analyzing historical data to identify patterns and lessons learned.

Threat Hunting: Threat hunting involves proactively searching for signs of malicious activity within an organization's environment. AI-powered threat intelligence supports threat hunting by providing advanced analytical tools and techniques. Machine learning algorithms can analyze large datasets to identify subtle indicators of compromise that may not be detected by traditional methods. For example, these frameworks can uncover hidden patterns or anomalous behaviors that suggest the presence of a sophisticated threat actor. By leveraging AI in threat hunting, organizations can enhance their ability to detect and address advanced threats before they cause significant harm.

Benefits and Drawbacks of AI-Powered Threat Intelligence

As every concept offers tremendous results, it is also imperative to examine the disadvantages as well. This gives a holistic view of the workings of the concept. Here are some of the benefits of using this technology to drive threat intelligence.

Improved Accuracy and Efficiency: It improves the accuracy and efficiency of threat detection and analysis. Machine learning algorithms can process and analyze vast amounts of data quickly, identifying relevant threat indicators and patterns with greater precision than manual methods. This enhanced accuracy reduces the likelihood of false positives and false negatives, allowing security teams to focus on genuine threats and respond more effectively. Additionally, AI-driven automation streamlines data aggregation and analysis processes, freeing up analysts to focus on more strategic tasks.

Scalability: One of the significant advantages of AI-powered threat intelligence is its scalability. As the volume of threat data continues to grow, AI systems can scale to handle larger datasets and more complex analyses. Machine learning algorithms can adapt to increasing data volumes and evolving threat landscapes, providing continuous and comprehensive threat intelligence. This scalability ensures that organizations can effectively manage and respond to the growing number of threats without being overwhelmed by the sheer volume of data.

Proactive Defense: It enables a more proactive defense posture by identifying and addressing potential threats before they materialize. Predictive analytics and advanced analysis techniques allow organizations to anticipate emerging threats and vulnerabilities, enabling them to implement preventive measures and strengthen their defenses. By staying ahead of potential risks, organizations can reduce the likelihood of successful attacks and minimize the impact of security incidents.

Its Challenges and Limitations include:

Data Privacy and Security: The aggregation and analysis of large volumes of data raise concerns about data privacy and security. AI systems must handle sensitive information responsibly, ensuring that data is anonymized, encrypted, and protected against unauthorized access. Organizations must comply with data protection regulations, such as GDPR or CCPA, and implement robust security measures to safeguard data used in threat intelligence.

False Positives and False Negatives: AI-powered threat intelligence systems can generate false positives (incorrectly identifying benign activities as threats) and false negatives (failing to detect actual threats). Balancing sensitivity and specificity is crucial to minimizing these issues. While AI algorithms improve accuracy over time, they may still require ongoing tuning and adjustment to reduce the occurrence of false positives and false negatives.

Complexity and Integration: Integrating this framework with existing security infrastructure can be complex and resource-intensive. Organizations must ensure compatibility between these systems and their current security tools, processes, and workflows. Additionally, deploying and maintaining AI-driven solutions may require specialized expertise and significant investment. Overcoming these challenges is essential to realizing the full benefits of AI in threat intelligence.

Future trends in AI-powered threat intelligence are poised to further transform cybersecurity by integrating advanced technologies and evolving practices. The rise of more sophisticated AI models will enhance real-time threat detection and response capabilities, providing deeper insights into emerging threats and attack vectors. Increased integration with other technologies, such as security orchestration and automation (SOAR) platforms, will enable more streamlined and effective security operations. There will also be a stronger emphasis on ethical AI practices and data privacy, ensuring that these systems are developed and used responsibly. As it continues to advance, we can expect greater emphasis on adaptive and autonomous threat detection systems, which will enhance predictive capabilities and proactive defense strategies, ultimately leading to a more resilient security landscape.

To fully maximize the potential of any mechanism, it is essential to evaluate the effectiveness and how discovered areas of weaknesses can be improved upon. There are key metrics for assessing the AI-powered threat intelligence platform.

Accuracy and Precision: One of the primary metrics for evaluating these solutions is accuracy. This refers to the system's ability to correctly identify genuine threats while minimizing false positives (benign activities flagged as threats) and false negatives (actual threats not detected). Precision, a related metric, measures the proportion of true positive detections relative to the total number of detections. High accuracy and precision are critical for ensuring that threat intelligence systems provide reliable insights and avoid overwhelming security teams with false alerts.

Response Time: Response time is another crucial metric, reflecting how quickly the AI system can detect, analyze, and alert on potential threats. Rapid response is essential for minimizing the window of opportunity for attackers and reducing the potential impact of threats. Effective AI-powered solutions should provide real-time or near-real-time alerts, enabling security teams to act swiftly and mitigate risks before they escalate. Measuring response time helps assess the efficiency of the system in identifying and addressing threats.

Coverage and Scope: The coverage and scope of a solution refer to the breadth of threat data sources and the range of threats it can identify. A comprehensive solution should aggregate data from various sources, including internal security logs, external threat feeds, and dark web sources, and cover a wide range of threat types. Evaluating coverage and scope involves assessing the system's ability to detect both known and emerging threats across different attack vectors and environments. A broad and deep coverage ensures that the threat intelligence system provides a holistic view of the threat landscape.

Incident Reduction and Mitigation: Evaluating the impact of this framework involves measuring their effectiveness in reducing the number and severity of security incidents. This includes assessing how well the system contributes to incident prevention, detection, and mitigation. Key indicators of impact include a reduction in successful attacks, a decrease in response times, and improved incident resolution rates. By analyzing historical incident data before and after the implementation of AI solutions, organizations can gauge the value added by the system in enhancing their overall security posture.

Cost-Benefit Analysis: Conducting a cost-benefit analysis helps determine the financial value of AI-powered threat intelligence solutions relative to their cost. This involves evaluating the direct costs of implementing and maintaining the system, such as licensing fees, infrastructure, and personnel training, against the benefits gained, including improved threat detection, reduced incident response times, and minimized financial losses from security breaches. A positive cost-benefit ratio indicates that the investment in AI-powered threat intelligence is justified and delivers tangible value to the organization.

User Satisfaction and Usability: User satisfaction and usability are important factors in assessing the effectiveness of this mechanism. Evaluating user feedback and experiences can provide insights into the system's ease of use, integration with existing workflows, and overall effectiveness. Metrics such as user satisfaction surveys, system adoption rates, and feedback on the usability of the interface and features help identify strengths and areas for improvement. Ensuring that the system is user-friendly and meets the needs of security professionals is essential for maximizing its effectiveness.

Regular Performance Reviews: Regular performance reviews are crucial for maintaining and enhancing the effectiveness of AI-powered threat intelligence solutions. These reviews involve analyzing system performance data, reviewing incident outcomes, and assessing the accuracy and relevance of threat intelligence provided by the system. Continuous monitoring and evaluation help identify trends, detect issues, and implement necessary adjustments to improve performance. Regular performance reviews ensure that the system remains effective in addressing evolving threats and adapting to changes in the threat landscape.

Updating Models and Data Sources: To ensure the continued effectiveness of this technology, it is essential to update models and data sources regularly. This includes retraining machine learning models with new threat data, incorporating feedback from incident analyses, and expanding data sources to cover emerging threats. Regular updates help maintain the system's accuracy, relevance, and ability to detect new attack vectors. Organizations should establish processes for continuous model improvement and data integration to keep the threat intelligence system aligned with current threats and trends.

Incorporating Feedback and Lessons Learned: Incorporating feedback and lessons learned from security incidents and user experiences is vital for refining AI-powered threat intelligence solutions. Organizations should actively seek input from security teams, incident response experts, and end-users to identify areas for improvement and address any shortcomings. Analyzing lessons learned from past incidents can provide valuable insights into system performance and highlight opportunities for enhancement. By integrating feedback and lessons learned, organizations can continuously improve their threat intelligence capabilities and better address evolving threats.

Case Study: Evaluating an AI-Powered Threat Intelligence Solution

Background and Objectives: In this case study, we examine the evaluation of an AI-powered threat intelligence solution implemented by a large financial institution. The primary objectives of the evaluation were to assess the system's accuracy, response time, and overall impact on security operations.

Evaluation Process and Findings: The evaluation involved analyzing key metrics such as false positive rates, response times, and the reduction in security incidents. The institution conducted a cost-benefit analysis to compare the costs of the system with the benefits gained in terms of improved threat detection and reduced incident response times. User satisfaction surveys and feedback were collected to assess the system's usability and effectiveness.

Results and Recommendations: The evaluation revealed that the AI-powered threat intelligence solution significantly improved threat detection accuracy and reduced response times. The cost-benefit analysis demonstrated a favorable return on investment, with notable reductions in security incidents and associated costs. User feedback indicated high satisfaction with the system's usability and integration with existing workflows. Recommendations included ongoing updates to threat models and data sources and regular performance reviews to ensure continued effectiveness.

Evaluating the effectiveness of these solutions involves assessing key metrics such as accuracy, response time, and coverage, as well as analyzing the impact on incident reduction and overall value. Continuous improvement through regular performance reviews, model updates, and feedback integration is essential for maintaining and enhancing the system's effectiveness. By employing a comprehensive evaluation approach, organizations can ensure that the technology provide maximum value and contribute to a robust security posture.

AI-powered threat intelligence represents a significant advancement in the field of cybersecurity, offering enhanced capabilities for aggregating and analyzing threat data. By leveraging AI for real-time threat detection, predictive analytics, and advanced analysis techniques, organizations can improve their ability to identify and mitigate zero-day exploits and other advanced threats. While challenges related to data privacy, false positives, and integration remain, the benefits of AI in threat intelligence are substantial, including improved accuracy, scalability, and proactive defense.

9. ETHICAL AND PRIVACY CONCERNS: BALANCING AI WITH USER RIGHTS

In recent years, artificial intelligence (AI) has increasingly become a force to reckon with across various sectors, from healthcare and finance to transportation and entertainment. Its potential to enhance industries and enhance human capabilities is immense. However, as AI systems become more integrated into everyday life, significant ethical and privacy concerns have emerged. Here we will learn the balance between leveraging the benefits of AI and upholding user rights, focusing on ethical considerations, privacy implications, and potential strategies for achieving equilibrium.

Understanding AI and Its Capabilities

AI encompasses a broad range of technologies designed to simulate human intelligence. These technologies include machine learning, natural language processing, and computer vision, among others. AI systems are capable of analyzing vast amounts of data, recognizing patterns, and making decisions with minimal human intervention. This capability drives innovation but also raises questions about how these systems should be used responsibly.

There are ethical and privacy concerns in the deployment of this technology and its interaction with human beings. One of the most pressing ethical concerns in AI is bias. These systems learn from historical data, which can reflect existing prejudices and inequalities. If not properly managed, these biases can perpetuate and even exacerbate discrimination. For example, algorithms used in hiring processes might favor candidates from certain demographic groups over others, reflecting biases present in the training data. To address this, developers must implement fairness-aware algorithms and continuously monitor AI systems for discriminatory outcomes. Additionally, diverse teams should be involved in the design and deployment phases to ensure a broad range of perspectives is considered.

Another is accountability and transparency in its decision-making process. The processes are often opaque, making it difficult to understand how outcomes are generated. This lack of transparency can undermine trust and accountability. For instance, if an AI system erroneously denies a loan or a medical diagnosis, the affected individuals may find it challenging to understand or contest the decision. To mitigate these issues, there is a growing call for "explainable AI" (XAI), which aims to make AI systems' decisions more understandable to non-experts. Establishing clear lines of accountability is also crucial, ensuring that organizations can be held responsible for the actions and decisions of their system. As these frameworks become more autonomous, concerns arise about the erosion of human control. For example, autonomous weapons or surveillance systems can make life-and-death decisions without human intervention. This raises ethical questions about the extent to which humans should delegate control to machines and the potential consequences of such delegations. Regulations and guidelines are needed to define acceptable levels of autonomy and ensure that human oversight remains a key component in critical decision-making processes.

These systems have the capacity to influence and manipulate human behavior, often in subtle ways. For instance, recommendation algorithms used by social media platforms can shape users' opinions, preferences, and behaviors by promoting certain content over others. This capability can be exploited for commercial gain, political manipulation, or even to spread misinformation. The ethical concern here revolves around the potential for AI systems to undermine individuals' autonomy by subtly influencing their choices and beliefs. Ensuring that the technologies are designed with safeguards to prevent manipulative practices is crucial. Developers and organizations should be transparent about the ways in which these systems influence user behavior and provide users with the ability to control their exposure to such influences.

Autonomous systems, such as self-driving cars or drones, present unique ethical challenges. Decisions made by these systems can have significant consequences for human safety and well-being. For example, in the event of an unavoidable accident, an autonomous vehicle may need to make a decision that involves sacrificing the safety of its occupants to protect pedestrians or other drivers. These scenarios raise complex ethical questions about how to program ethical decision-making into autonomous systems. The "trolley problem" is a well-known ethical dilemma in this context, where the system must choose between two harmful outcomes. Developing ethical guidelines and decision-making frameworks for autonomous systems is essential to ensure that they operate in a manner consistent with societal values and priorities.

Secondary use of data refers to the practice of using data for purposes other than those for which it was originally collected. AI systems often aggregate and analyze vast amounts of data, which can lead to the repurposing of personal information in ways that users did not anticipate or consent to. For example, data collected for improving user experience in one application might be used for targeted advertising or research without explicit user consent. This raises privacy concerns about the scope of data usage and the potential for data to be exploited in ways that infringe on individuals' expectations of privacy. To address this issue, organizations should implement clear data usage policies, provide transparent information about how data is used, and obtain explicit consent from users before repurposing their data.

These frameworks can generate inferences and predictions based on the data they analyze, which may reveal sensitive or private information about individuals. For example, predictive analytics used in healthcare or insurance can infer an individual's likelihood of developing a certain condition or their risk profile. These inferences can potentially lead to privacy breaches if they are used to make decisions about individuals without their knowledge or consent. The ethical concern here involves the potential misuse of inferred information and the impact it may have on individuals' privacy and autonomy. Organizations should establish clear guidelines for the use of predictive analytics and ensure that any inferences drawn from personal data are handled with the same level of care and confidentiality as the original data. Additionally, individuals should have the right to understand and contest inferences made about them.

Another privacy concern is data collection and surveillance. This technology often rely on large datasets, which can include personal information. The collection and analysis of this data can lead to extensive surveillance, where individuals' activities are monitored and analyzed without their explicit consent. This can infringe on privacy rights and lead to a loss of autonomy. To address this concerns, organizations should adopt data minimization principles, collecting only the data necessary for specific purposes. Also, robust consent mechanisms should be implemented, ensuring that individuals are aware of and agree to how their data is used. The security of personal data is paramount, especially as cyber threats become more sophisticated. AI systems can be vulnerable to breaches, which can expose sensitive information and compromise user privacy. Ensuring the security of data requires implementing strong encryption methods, regular security audits, and robust access controls. There are also inquires on who owns and controls data. These questions about who owns and controls personal data are central to privacy discussions. Individuals should have clear rights to their data, including the ability to access, correct, and delete information held by organizations. Legal frameworks like the General Data Protection Regulation (GDPR) provide guidelines for data ownership, but ongoing updates and enforcement are necessary to keep pace with technological advancements.

Balancing AI Use with User Rights

We have established that AI is a technology with tremendous opportunities and to maximize such, a balance between its application and user rights is paramount. There are several measures we can take to achieve this objective.

Regulatory Frameworks: Effective regulation is essential for balancing AI innovation with ethical and privacy considerations. Regulations should be designed to protect user rights while allowing for technological advancement. Frameworks like the GDPR have set important precedents, but additional regulations may be needed to address specific AI-related issues. Regulators must engage with technology experts, ethicists, and civil society to create balanced policies that reflect diverse perspectives and adapt to rapid technological changes.

Ethical AI Design: This design involves integrating ethical considerations into every stage of the development process. This includes conducting ethical impact assessments, engaging with stakeholders, and adopting best practices for fairness, transparency, and accountability. Organizations should foster a culture of ethical awareness and provide training for developers to recognize and address ethical dilemmas.

Public Engagement and Education: Public engagement is crucial for understanding and addressing AI's ethical and privacy concerns. Educating the public about the technologies, their potential impacts, and their rights can empower individuals to make informed decisions and advocate for their interests. Transparency and open communication between AI developers, organizations, and the public can build trust and ensure that these systems are developed and deployed responsibly.

Collaborative Approaches: Collaboration between governments, industry, academia, and civil society can facilitate the development of comprehensive strategies for managing AI's ethical and privacy challenges. Multi-stakeholder initiatives can provide diverse perspectives and expertise, leading to more robust and inclusive solutions.

Establishing Ethics Committees: Ethics committees play a crucial role in ensuring that AI technologies are developed and deployed in line with ethical standards. These committees, often comprised of ethicists, technologists, legal experts, and representatives from affected communities, provide oversight and guidance on AI projects. They are responsible for reviewing AI systems' potential impacts, identifying ethical dilemmas, and recommending best practices. Establishing ethics committees within organizations can help create a structured approach to addressing ethical issues. These committees should have the authority to halt or modify projects that pose significant ethical risks. Their work can include developing ethical guidelines, conducting impact assessments, and ensuring that AI systems align with organizational values and societal norms.

Governance Models for AI: Effective governance models are essential for managing the complexities of AI deployment. Governance frameworks should outline clear policies and procedures for the development, implementation, and monitoring of these systems. These frameworks can include principles for transparency, accountability, and user rights, as well as mechanisms for addressing grievances and disputes. Governance models can also involve setting up independent oversight bodies that monitor compliance with ethical standards and regulations. These bodies can conduct audits, review AI systems' performance, and ensure that organizations adhere to established guidelines. Collaboration between regulatory agencies, industry leaders, and academic institutions can enhance the effectiveness of governance models.

Ethical Training and Culture: Creating a culture of ethics within organizations is vital for fostering responsible AI development. Ethical training programs can educate employees about the potential risks and ethical considerations associated with AI. These programs should cover topics such as bias mitigation, data privacy, and the ethical implications of automation. Promoting an organizational culture that prioritizes ethical behavior involves encouraging open dialogue about ethical issues, rewarding ethical decision-making, and integrating ethics into performance evaluations. By embedding ethics into the organizational fabric, companies can ensure that all members are aligned with the values of fairness, transparency, and respect for user rights.

Legal and Regulatory Frameworks for AI Ethics and Privacy

Existing Legal Frameworks: Current legal frameworks like the GDPR and the California Consumer Privacy Act (CCPA) provide important protections for user privacy and data security. These regulations set standards for data collection, consent, and user rights, addressing some of the privacy concerns associated with AI. They require organizations to be transparent about data practices and to give users control over their personal information. However, legal frameworks often struggle to keep pace with rapid technological advancements. As this technology evolves, existing laws may need to be updated or supplemented to address new challenges. For instance, regulations may need to address issues related to AI-generated content, deepfakes, or the use of AI in sensitive areas like healthcare or criminal justice.

Proposed Legislative Changes: To better address AI-specific concerns, there are ongoing efforts to develop new legislative measures. For example, the European Union's proposed AI Act aims to create a comprehensive regulatory framework for AI, focusing on high-risk applications and ensuring that these systems meet strict requirements for transparency, accountability, and safety. Proposed legislative changes often involve input from various stakeholders, including industry experts, civil rights advocates, and policymakers. These changes aim to strike a balance between fostering innovation and protecting individual rights. Engaging in public consultations and impact assessments can help shape effective and adaptable legal frameworks.

International Cooperation and Standards: AI is a global technology, and addressing its ethical and privacy concerns requires international cooperation. Developing global standards and agreements can help ensure that these systems are governed consistently across borders. International organizations, such as the International Organization for Standardization (ISO) and the Institute of Electrical and Electronics Engineers (IEEE), are working on standards related to AI ethics and privacy. Collaboration between countries and international bodies can promote best practices and facilitate knowledge sharing. Creating a common regulatory framework or aligning national regulations can help address cross-border issues and prevent regulatory arbitrage, where companies move operations to jurisdictions with less stringent rules.

The Impact of AI on Social Justice and Equity

The integration of these technologies into various sectors raises critical questions about their impact on social justice and equity. As AI systems increasingly influence decision-making processes, ensuring that they contribute to a fair and inclusive society becomes paramount.

AI and Social Inequality: These technologies have the potential to either alleviate or exacerbate social inequalities. For instance, AI-driven decision-making in areas such as lending, hiring, and criminal justice can perpetuate existing disparities if not carefully managed. Bias in AI algorithms can lead to discriminatory practices that disproportionately affect marginalized communities. Addressing these issues requires a focus on social justice and equity in AI design and deployment. Ensuring that these frameworks are fair and inclusive involves analyzing their impact on different demographic groups and implementing measures to mitigate any adverse effects. Engaging with community organizations and advocacy groups can provide valuable insights into the needs and concerns of affected populations.

Promoting Inclusive AI Development: To promote social justice, it is essential to include diverse voices in the development of AI technologies. This includes involving individuals from various socio-economic backgrounds, genders, races, and geographic regions in the design and implementation phases. Diverse teams are more likely to recognize and address potential biases and ensure that these systems are equitable and representative. Inclusive development also involves creating accessible technologies that benefit a wide range of users. Ensuring that the applications are designed with accessibility in mind can help bridge the digital divide and provide opportunities for underserved communities.

Supporting Fair Access to AI Benefits: Ensuring that the benefits of AI are distributed fairly is another crucial aspect of promoting social justice. This involves addressing issues related to the digital divide, where certain communities may have limited access to these technologies and their advantages. Initiatives to support education, training, and access to technology can help ensure that more people can benefit from AI advancements. Public and private sector partnerships can play a role in supporting equitable access to AI benefits. For example, programs that provide training and resources to underserved communities can help individuals gain the skills needed to participate in the economy.

Balancing the transformative potential of AI with the need to protect ethical principles and privacy rights is a complex but essential task. As these technologies continue to evolve, it is crucial to address concerns related to bias, accountability, transparency, and data privacy. By implementing effective regulations, fostering ethical AI design, engaging the public, and promoting collaborative approaches, we can harness the benefits of this technology while upholding the rights and values of individuals. Achieving this balance requires ongoing effort and vigilance, but it is necessary for ensuring that AI serves humanity in a fair, transparent, and respectful manner.

10. AI AND HUMAN COLLABORATION

Artificial Intelligence (AI) has revolutionized various domains, including defense, where its integration with traditional methods is transforming security strategies. The convergence of AI with human expertise in defense scenarios introduces a hybrid approach that leverages the strengths of both automated and manual strategies. This synergy aims to enhance effectiveness, agility, and precision in addressing complex and dynamic threats. This chapter will examine how AI and human collaboration can be optimized in defense strategies, examining the roles of automated and manual approaches, their combined impact on security, and the challenges and opportunities that arise from their integration.

AI and Human Functions in Defense Frameworks

It plays a tremendous role in defense by significantly enhancing efficiency, precision, and strategic capabilities. One of the key contributions of AI is its ability to automate routine tasks and processes, thereby increasing operational efficiency. For instance, AI systems can analyze vast amounts of data quickly, identify patterns, and detect anomalies with a level of speed and accuracy that surpasses traditional methods. This capability is particularly valuable in cybersecurity, where AI algorithms monitor network traffic and respond to potential threats in real-time, ensuring robust digital defenses.

Furthermore, it improves precision in decision-making by providing actionable insights through advanced data analysis and predictive analytics. In military operations, AI-driven simulations and predictions can forecast enemy movements and optimize resource allocation, aiding commanders in making informed and strategic decisions. The deployment of autonomous systems, such as drones and robotic vehicles, also exemplifies its role in performing tasks with high precision, whether for reconnaissance, surveillance, or direct engagement. It enhances situational awareness by integrating data from diverse sources, such as satellites, drones, and sensors, to deliver a comprehensive and current overview of the operational environment. This enriched situational awareness allows defense personnel to respond more effectively to threats and adapt strategies based on a thorough understanding of the dynamic landscape. AI also contributes to predictive maintenance and logistics by forecasting equipment failures and optimizing supply chains, which helps maintain operational readiness and reduce costs. Lastly, it strengthens cyber defense by detecting and mitigating threats more swiftly and accurately, thus safeguarding critical infrastructure from increasingly sophisticated cyber-attacks.

Enhanced situational awareness is a crucial benefit of AI in defense, achieved through the integration and analysis of data from diverse sources in real time. Advanced systems process inputs from satellite imagery, drones, sensors, and communication networks to deliver a comprehensive and current picture of the operational environment. This capability allows military and defense personnel to make better-informed decisions, respond more effectively to threats, and anticipate potential developments. By detecting subtle changes or emerging patterns that traditional methods might overlook, AI provides a strategic advantage in navigating dynamic and complex scenarios.

Predictive maintenance and logistics are significantly improved through the use of advanced technology in defense operations. Predictive maintenance involves analyzing data from equipment sensors and maintenance records to forecast potential failures before they occur. This proactive approach helps prevent equipment breakdowns, minimize downtime, and ensure that critical assets remain ready for use. In logistics, advanced systems optimize supply chain management by forecasting demand, streamlining inventory management, and enhancing the efficiency of distribution networks. These improvements not only enhance operational readiness but also help reduce costs by ensuring that resources are available and functioning as needed.

Similarly, cyber defense capabilities are markedly enhanced through sophisticated systems that improve real-time threat detection and response. By analyzing vast amounts of network traffic, these systems can quickly identify anomalies or potential cyber threats more efficiently than human operators. Machine learning algorithms within these systems detect patterns indicative of malicious activities, such as phishing attempts or malware infections, and can automatically respond to mitigate risks. These systems adapt to evolving threats by continuously learning from new attack vectors and adjusting defense strategies accordingly. This adaptive capability strengthens overall cyber resilience and provides robust protection for critical infrastructure against increasingly sophisticated cyber-attacks.

Human expertise remains indispensable in defense due to its unique contributions to strategic thinking, adaptability, and ethical oversight. While AI systems excel at processing data and performing repetitive tasks, human operators bring crucial strategic insight and adaptability to complex scenarios. Their ability to understand and interpret nuanced contextual factors such as political, cultural, and psychological elements enables them to make informed decisions that go beyond data-driven insights. Furthermore, humans are essential for overseeing these systems to address ethical considerations and ensure responsible use. They can identify and correct biases in AI algorithms, ensuring that these systems operate fairly and transparently. Additionally, human operators handle crisis management with emotional resilience and leadership, managing high-stress situations and providing support to personnel in ways that these systems cannot. By integrating human judgment with AI capabilities, defense strategies benefit from both advanced technological analysis and the invaluable qualities of human experience and oversight.

Human expertise plays a vital role in driving creativity and innovation within defense strategies. While AI systems excel at processing data and identifying patterns, humans are uniquely capable of thinking creatively and devising novel solutions to complex problems. For example, in strategic planning or counter-terrorism operations, human ingenuity can generate innovative tactics and approaches that might not occur to AI systems. Analysts can envision various scenarios, anticipate unconventional threats, and develop new methods to tackle emerging challenges. This capacity for creative problem-solving is essential for adapting to rapidly evolving threats and maintaining effective defense strategies in a dynamic environment.

It is crucial for understanding and navigating the interpersonal and cultural dynamics that influence defense operations. In scenarios such as international relations, peacekeeping missions, or local engagements, human operators excel at interpreting cultural nuances, building relationships, and fostering cooperation with diverse stakeholders. While these systems are adept at data analysis, they lack the ability to fully grasp human emotions, cultural contexts, and social interactions. This expertise ensures that defense strategies remain sensitive to these factors, promoting effective communication and positive outcomes in complex and varied environments.

Similarly, during crises or high-stress situations, human expertise is essential for managing the emotional and psychological aspects that AI systems cannot address. Humans bring emotional resilience, the ability to make decisions under pressure, and the capability to provide leadership and support during emergencies. In combat scenarios or disaster response, leaders must navigate emotionally charged situations, motivate their teams, and support personnel facing extreme conditions. While this technology contributes valuable data-driven insights and automation, they cannot replicate the emotional intelligence and psychological strength required for effective crisis management. Thus, human operators are indispensable in ensuring that defense strategies account for these critical human dimensions, maintaining operational effectiveness and supporting the well-being of all involved.

Synergizing AI and Human Strategies

Synergizing AI and human strategies create a powerful approach to modern defense, combining the analytical prowess of AI with the strategic insight of human expertise. This integration maximizes effectiveness by leveraging the strengths of both automated systems and human judgment to navigate complex and dynamic security challenges through the following ways:

Complementary Strengths: The synergy between these two components lies in their complementary strengths. AI systems provide speed, precision, and data-driven insights, while human operators offer strategic thinking, ethical judgment, and adaptability. By integrating these strengths, defense strategies can achieve a higher level of effectiveness and resilience. For example, in cybersecurity, these frameworks can handle routine threat detection and response tasks, allowing human analysts to focus on more complex and strategic aspects of security management. This division of labor enhances overall efficiency and effectiveness, ensuring that both automated and manual strategies contribute to a robust defense posture.

Collaboration and Integration: Effective collaboration between AI and human operators requires seamless integration of technologies and workflows. This involves designing structures that complement human capabilities rather than replace them. User interfaces should be intuitive, and decision support tools should enhance rather than overwhelm human judgment. Training programs are essential to ensure that human operators can effectively interact with the systems created. This includes understanding AI outputs, interpreting data, and making informed decisions based on both automated and manual inputs. Regular updates and feedback loops between AI systems and human operators help refine processes and improve collaboration.

Scenario-Based Applications: The integration of the concepts can be illustrated through various scenario-based applications. In military operations, for instance, AI can assist in planning and executing complex missions by providing real-time data and simulations. Human commanders can use this information to make strategic decisions, adapt to changing conditions, and coordinate with allied forces. In disaster response and recovery, these systems can analyze data from multiple sources to predict and manage crises. Human responders can leverage these insights to prioritize resources, coordinate efforts, and provide on-the-ground support. The synergy between AI's analytical capabilities and human expertise ensures a more effective and coordinated response.

Adaptive Learning and Continuous Improvement: It enables adaptive learning and continuous improvement in defense operations. AI systems can learn from the outcomes of past operations, analyze feedback, and refine their algorithms to enhance performance over time. Human operators contribute by providing contextual feedback, interpreting their insights, and making adjustments based on real-world experiences. This iterative process ensures that both AI systems and human strategies evolve in response to new information, emerging threats, and changing operational conditions. By leveraging its capacity for adaptive learning alongside human expertise, defense strategies can become more effective and resilient.

Scenario Simulation and Training: AI and human collaboration enhances scenario simulation and training for defense personnel. These simulation tools can create realistic and complex training environments by generating dynamic scenarios based on historical data, threat models, and operational variables. These simulations allow personnel to practice responses and decision-making in a controlled setting, improving their readiness for real-world situations. Human trainers and strategists can use these simulations to assess and refine tactics, provide targeted feedback, and ensure that training aligns with actual defense needs. This combination of AI-driven simulations and human oversight enhances the effectiveness of training programs and prepares defense forces for a wide range of scenarios.

Augmented Decision-Making: The collaboration between AI and human strategies enhances decision-making by combining the computational power of automated systems with human judgment. In both defense and cyber defense, AI rapidly processes and analyzes vast amounts of data to provide valuable insights and recommendations. For instance, in military planning, it offers data-driven analysis on various strategic options, while human commanders use their experience and contextual understanding to make final decisions. Similarly, in cybersecurity, automated systems help identify potential threats and vulnerabilities, but human analysts interpret these findings and implement effective responses. This approach ensures a more informed and balanced decision-making process by leveraging both advanced analytics and human expertise.

Integrating AI with human strategies in defense presents both significant challenges and valuable opportunities. One major challenge is ensuring the reliability and fairness of AI systems, as biases in data or algorithms can lead to skewed outcomes that affect decision-making. Continuous monitoring and updating of the models are essential to address these issues and maintain their accuracy. Another challenge is the risk of over-reliance on the technology, which could lead to reduced human vigilance and critical thinking. Balancing automation with active human oversight is crucial to prevent complacency and ensure that human judgment remains central to strategic decisions.

Despite these challenges, the synergy between AI and human expertise offers numerous opportunities. AI can handle routine tasks and provide data-driven insights, allowing human operators to focus on more complex and strategic aspects of defense operations. This division of labor enhances overall efficiency and effectiveness. Also, the integration of its structures drives innovation, leading to the development of new tools and methodologies that can advance defense capabilities. Collaborative efforts in research and development can result in sophisticated AI systems that complement human skills, improving readiness and resilience across various defense domains. By navigating the challenges and embracing the opportunities, the collaboration between AI and human strategies can lead to more robust and adaptable defense systems.

The synergy between AI and human collaboration represents a powerful approach to modern defense strategies. By combining the strengths of automated systems with human expertise, defense organizations can achieve greater efficiency, precision, and adaptability. However, addressing challenges such as system reliability and potential over-reliance is crucial to maximizing the benefits of this collaboration.

As it continues to progress, ongoing research, training, and integration efforts will be essential to ensuring that AI and human strategies work together effectively. By leveraging the complementary strengths of both strategies, defense strategies can become more robust, responsive, and aligned with ethical and strategic objectives. The future of defense lies in harnessing the potential of AI while maintaining the irreplaceable value of human judgment and oversight.

11. INTEGRATING AI INTO CYBER DEFENSE:
KEY TAKEAWAYS AND FUTURE DIRECTIONS

The integration of artificial intelligence (AI) into cybersecurity represents a profound shift in how we approach digital threats and safeguard information systems. This final chapter summarizes the key insights from the book, reflecting on how AI is reshaping cyber defense, and explores future trends and directions for ongoing advancements in the field. Drawing on the various chapters discussed throughout the book, this chapter provides a comprehensive overview of AI's role in advancing cybersecurity, highlights practical applications and case studies, and outlines potential future developments.

Key Takeaways

AI's Transformative Impact on Cyber Defense

One of the most significant takeaways from the book is the transformative impact of AI on cyber defense. AI technologies, particularly machine learning (ML) and deep learning, have revolutionized threat detection and response. AI-driven threat detection enhances security by analyzing vast amounts of data to identify patterns and anomalies that might indicate a potential threat.

This capability allows for more proactive and accurate identification of malicious activities compared to traditional methods.

For instance, machine learning algorithms can analyze network traffic and user behavior to detect unusual patterns that could signify a breach or an attempted attack. This real-time analysis enables quicker and more precise responses, significantly improving the overall security posture of an organization. The ability of AI systems to adapt and learn from new data ensures that they remain effective in the face of evolving threats.

Automating Incident Response

Automating incident response is another crucial advancement discussed in the book. AI systems can automate routine security tasks, such as alerting, log analysis, and initial response actions. This automation not only speeds up the reaction time but also reduces the likelihood of human error, which can be critical in high-stress situations. For example, AI-powered incident response systems can automatically isolate affected systems, block suspicious IP addresses, and initiate predefined countermeasures without human intervention. This rapid response capability minimizes damage and helps organizations recover more quickly from security incidents. The integration of this technology into incident response also allows security teams to focus on more complex tasks, such as strategic decision-making and long-term threat analysis.

Behavioral Analysis and Anomaly Detection

Behavioral analysis and anomaly detection are pivotal applications of AI in cybersecurity. These systems use advanced algorithms to analyze normal user and network behavior, establishing a baseline against which deviations can be detected. This approach is particularly effective in identifying insider threats and sophisticated attacks that might bypass traditional signature-based detection systems.

By leveraging AI for behavioral analysis, organizations can detect subtle changes in user behavior or system activity that may indicate a breach. For instance, this security system might identify unusual login patterns or data access behaviors that deviate from established norms, flagging these as potential threats. This proactive detection capability enhances an organization's ability to respond to emerging threats before they escalate into more significant issues.

Predictive Analytics for Anticipating Attacks

Predictive analytics is another area where AI demonstrates its value in cybersecurity. These tools analyze historical data and current threat trends to forecast potential future attacks. By identifying patterns and trends, AI can help organizations anticipate and prepare for new types of cyber threats.

For example, predictive analytics can be used to assess the likelihood of specific attack vectors based on historical data and emerging threat intelligence. This forward-looking approach allows organizations to implement preventive measures and strengthen their defenses against anticipated threats. By employing predictive analytics, security teams can stay ahead of adversaries and reduce the likelihood of successful attacks.

Mitigating Zero-Day Exploits

The role of AI in identifying and mitigating zero-day exploits is another key takeaway. Zero-day exploits, which target previously unknown vulnerabilities, pose significant challenges for traditional security measures. These systems can help address this challenge by identifying suspicious activities and patterns that might indicate the presence of a zero-day exploit. AI-driven security tools can analyze software behavior and network traffic for signs of anomalous activity that could suggest an unknown vulnerability being exploited. This early detection capability is crucial for mitigating the impact of zero-day exploits and ensuring that security patches and updates are applied in a timely manner.

AI-Powered Threat Intelligence

AI's role in threat intelligence is transformative, as it enables the aggregation and analysis of vast amounts of data to enhance overall security. AI-powered threat intelligence platforms can process data from multiple sources, including threat feeds, social media, and dark web forums, to provide actionable insights into emerging threats and vulnerabilities. By aggregating and analyzing diverse data sources, it can help organizations stay informed about the latest threat trends and adjust their security strategies accordingly. This comprehensive view of the threat landscape allows for more effective threat detection and response, ensuring that organizations are better prepared to defend against a wide range of cyber threats.

Ethical and Privacy Concerns

The integration of AI into cybersecurity also raises important ethical and privacy concerns. Balancing the benefits of AI-driven security with the need to protect user privacy and uphold ethical standards is a critical consideration. Ensuring that the systems are designed and implemented in a way that respects user rights and avoids biases is essential for maintaining trust and effectiveness.

The book discusses the need for transparent AI practices, including clear guidelines for data collection, usage, and retention. Addressing these ethical concerns helps ensure that the systems enhance security without compromising individual privacy or reinforcing existing biases.

Practical Applications of AI in Cyber Defense

The practical applications of AI in cyber defense have revolutionized how organizations approach security challenges, offering tangible improvements in threat detection, response, and management. By leveraging these technologies, organizations can address a wide range of security issues more effectively and efficiently. This section explores several key practical applications of AI in the field, highlighting real-world implementations and their impact on enhancing cybersecurity measures.

Real-Time Threat Detection and Monitoring: Its capability for real-time threat detection and monitoring is one of its most impactful applications in cyber defense. Traditional security systems often rely on predefined signatures and rules, which can be ineffective against novel or sophisticated attacks. AI-driven systems, however, use machine learning algorithms to analyze network traffic and user behavior in real time, identifying anomalies that may indicate a potential threat. For example, AI-powered Security Information and Event Management (SIEM) systems continuously monitor data from various sources, such as firewalls, intrusion detection systems, and endpoint security solutions. By analyzing patterns and correlating events, these systems can detect unusual activities such as sudden spikes in network traffic or irregular login attempts that might signal a security breach. The ability to identify and respond to threats in real time allows organizations to mitigate risks before they escalate into more serious issues.

Automated Incident Response: Automated incident response is another critical application of AI in cybersecurity. When a potential threat is detected, these systems can automatically trigger predefined responses to contain and mitigate the attack. This automation reduces the time required to address incidents and minimizes the potential damage caused by cyber threats. For example, AI-driven security solutions can automatically isolate compromised systems from the network, block malicious IP addresses, and apply security patches without human intervention. This rapid response capability is particularly valuable in environments with high volumes of alerts and limited human resources. By automating routine responses, organizations can ensure a swift and consistent approach to incident management, while human analysts focus on more complex tasks and strategic decision-making.

Behavioral Analytics and Insider Threat Detection: AI's role in behavioral analytics and insider threat detection provides significant benefits for identifying and addressing internal security risks. Unlike conventional methods that rely on static rules, these frameworks use machine learning to establish baseline behaviors for users and systems. By continuously monitoring for deviations from these baselines, it can detect suspicious activities that might indicate an insider threat. For instance, AI-powered systems can identify unusual access patterns, such as employees accessing sensitive data outside their usual scope of work or exhibiting atypical login times. These deviations can trigger alerts for further investigation by security teams. This approach helps organizations detect and respond to insider threats more effectively, reducing the risk of data breaches and other security incidents caused by malicious or negligent insiders.

Enhanced Threat Intelligence and Analysis: It enhances threat intelligence and analysis by aggregating and analyzing data from diverse sources, including threat feeds, social media, and dark web forums. AI-powered threat intelligence platforms can identify emerging threats, track the activities of known adversaries, and provide actionable insights for strengthening defenses. For example, these systems can analyze patterns in malware samples, track the infrastructure used by cybercriminals, and correlate these findings with global threat trends. This comprehensive analysis helps organizations stay informed about the latest threats and vulnerabilities, allowing them to adapt their security strategies accordingly. By integrating AI for threat intelligence, organizations can proactively address potential risks and improve their overall security posture.

Phishing Detection and Prevention: AI has made significant strides in improving phishing detection and prevention, a common and highly effective attack vector used by cybercriminals. Phishing attacks often involve deceptive emails or messages designed to trick users into revealing sensitive information or downloading malicious software. AI systems can analyze email content, sender reputation, and other factors to identify potential phishing attempts. For example, AI-powered email filters can assess the characteristics of incoming messages, such as language patterns, hyperlinks, and attachments, to detect signs of phishing. Machine learning algorithms can continuously learn from new phishing tactics and adapt their detection capabilities accordingly. This proactive approach helps reduce the likelihood of successful phishing attacks and protects users from falling victim to these deceptive schemes.

Vulnerability Management and Patch Management: It assists in vulnerability management and patch management by automating the identification and prioritization of security vulnerabilities. AI systems can analyze software and system configurations to identify potential weaknesses that could be exploited by attackers. By assessing the risk and impact of each vulnerability, it can help organizations prioritize remediation efforts more effectively. For instance, AI-driven vulnerability management tools can scan systems for known vulnerabilities, assess their severity, and provide recommendations for patching. By automating this process, organizations can ensure that critical vulnerabilities are addressed promptly and reduce the window of opportunity for attackers. This proactive approach to vulnerability management enhances overall security and helps prevent successful exploits.

Future Directions

1. Advancements in AI Algorithms: Looking ahead, advancements in AI algorithms are likely to drive significant improvements in cybersecurity. Continued research and development in machine learning and deep learning techniques will enhance the capabilities of

the systems, allowing them to detect and respond to increasingly sophisticated threats. Innovations in these algorithms will also improve the accuracy of threat detection and reduce false positives, leading to more effective security measures.

2. Integration with Emerging Technologies: The integration with emerging technologies, such as blockchain and quantum computing, represents a promising direction for the future of cybersecurity. Blockchain technology can enhance data integrity and transparency, while quantum computing has the potential to revolutionize cryptographic techniques. Combining AI with these technologies could lead to more robust and secure defense mechanisms.

3. Human-AI Collaboration: The future will increasingly rely on effective collaboration between AI and human experts. While AI systems will continue to provide valuable insights and automation, human judgment and expertise will remain essential for interpreting data, making strategic decisions, and addressing ethical considerations. Developing effective human-AI collaboration strategies will be crucial for maximizing the benefits of AI while maintaining a balanced and ethical approach to cybersecurity.

4. Regulatory and Compliance Considerations: As AI becomes more integrated into security frameworks, regulatory and compliance considerations will become increasingly important. Ensuring that AI systems comply with industry standards and regulations will be essential for maintaining security and protecting user privacy. Developing and implementing regulatory frameworks that address the unique challenges of AI will be a key focus for future advancements.

5. Enhanced Training and Education: Finally, enhanced training and education will be vital for preparing cybersecurity professionals to work effectively with AI systems. As the technology continues to evolve, it will be important for security experts to stay updated on the latest advancements and best practices. Investing in training programs and educational initiatives will help ensure that professionals are equipped with the knowledge and skills needed to leverage AI effectively and ethically in their defense strategies.

The integration of AI into cyber defense has already demonstrated its potential, offering significant advancements in threat detection, incident response, and predictive analytics. However, as we look to the future, ongoing advancements in AI technology, coupled with effective human-AI collaboration, will continue to shape the landscape of cybersecurity. Addressing ethical and privacy concerns, exploring new technologies, and investing in training and education will be essential for maximizing the benefits of AI while maintaining a secure and ethical approach to defending against cyber threats. By embracing these opportunities and navigating the associated challenges, we can build a more resilient and adaptive cybersecurity framework for the future.

ABOUT THE AUTHOR

With years of extensive experience in cybersecurity within telecommunications, MSSP, and the fitness/hospitality sectors, Stephen Nnamdi is a seasoned Cyber Security Analyst dedicated to delivering high-caliber security solutions and risk management.

He possesses deep expertise in Security Operations Center (SOC) analysis, vulnerability management, and data leak prevention (DLP). Proficient in a variety of security tools and technologies including intrusion prevention systems (IPS), endpoint DLP solutions, and SIEM platforms such as AlienVault and IBM QRadar.

Complemented by exceptional communication skills, he excels in conveying complex security concepts through detailed reports, presentations, and client interactions. His experience also includes drafting daily service reports, engaging with third-party vendors, and creating documentation and training materials.

When he is not immersing himself in professional engagements, Stephen pursues his hobbies and gives back to his community.